HOW TO GET
THE WOMAN OF YOUR DREAMS
USING THE INTERNET

Sebastian Chance

How to Get the Woman of Your Dreams Using the Internet

Published by Iceni Books®
610 East Delano Street, Suite 104
Tucson, Arizona 85705 U.S.A.
www.icenibooks.com

International Standard Book Number: 1-58736-402-6
Library of Congress Control Number: 2004113872

Dedication

This book is a direct result of my ex-fiancée taking a wonderful relationship of two years, and then throwing it all away without any real form of reasoning. But in the end it proved to be the best event of my life, because it allowed me to search and find the woman of my dreams. This book was written to help other men like me and give them the tools necessary to find the woman they are searching for. I hope by reading this book they can use the methods I did, without making all the mistakes I have along the way. And I hope they have the same outcome as me: Now I'm very much in love and plan to marry Lili, a wonderful woman I found in China. She is everything a man could ever want, and everything I will ever need. I love you with all my heart, Lili, for without you life for me would not exist.

Special thanks go out to Irshad Ali, Frederick Buike, and Gordon Day, for taking the time to read this book and make sure it was easy to follow and very understandable for the reader, and also to see that it had everything to ensure success for any man wanting to achieve happiness with a woman.

Special dedication: To the one person who has had the greatest influence on my life, the one who has shown me how to be the best that I can be. Without her guidance and love I would have never achieved what I have or turned out to be the man that I am today. Mom, I love you with all the love a son can give, and I will always be indebted to you for the things you taught me about love and the love that you have shared with me. It was this love that guided me in my search for true happiness.

CONTENTS

Introduction

So! You've decided it's time for a change; you want a woman in your life who will be with you forever. You're tired of the wrong types of women you're finding out there, and you have given up looking for something that doesn't seem to exist.

Or maybe you just want to see the world, or even different parts of the United States, and want to have a woman waiting for you upon your arrival in each destination. Until now this has been something many men have searched for, and yet they seem to have settled for whatever they ended up with, or even put off the trip because of lack of companionship.

It's time to stop this way of thinking and make a positive change for yourself. Finally you've decided that you will control your happiness. Now, you make the final decision of what type of woman you will spend your life with. Or even better yet, have one waiting for you, anticipating your arrival, who will show you around and make your trip unbelievable. There are millions of beautiful and eligible women out there waiting to be yours and yours only, but you have to take the initiative to do what is necessary to bring them into your life, and only you can make this dream a reality.

This book will walk you through every step necessary. The techniques have been tried and proven to provide men with women they thought didn't exist anywhere in the world. The techniques will help you find the sort of woman you thought you would never have the chance to meet, let alone marry.

You will learn what to look for, what types of women are available, how to pick a dating site and set up your profile. You will also learn how to make the perfect opener so the women will respond to you. Later, you'll find a step-by-step on how to meet her and get her back with you to the United States, including information on travel visas. We'll also discuss the scams that are out there, alerting you to their warning signs so you don't lose any of your hard-earned money. You will learn everything you need to know to make your search successful. And your love life will be everything you ever wanted.

The only thing you must do is carefully apply the steps in this text. This will help you get any woman on this planet who is looking for the same things as you. Does this mean strictly for marriage? No! Use these methods for whatever you want out of a relationship; the result is always up to you. But with these women you'll never need to worry about them cheating, or not wanting you to be with them. And they will love you and make you happy for the rest of your life.

You've decided once and for all that you will be happy, and you've bought this book to find out how to make these things happen. After you're finished, you will see that just by adapting the methods in this book to your own personality you can forever change your life.

I know you're asking yourself, does this really work? Well, for me it was amazing. I decided to write this book because of my many successes and all the things I learned along the way.

I spent a lot of money needlessly and was taken a few times by scams. I knew, after all that I went through, there were surely men out there just like me who were unaware of these methods; I also knew they didn't want to lose money or make the same mistakes I did. At the time I decided to write this book, I had women all over the world waiting for me to come to meet and possibly marry them. This method was the best way I have found to be selective, and pick the perfect wife for me. I now have girlfriends, so to speak, in various countries of the world—all this for a forty-year-old man. The ladies I have contacted and who have responded to me are all no older then twenty-three and live in such parts of the world as China, Ukraine, Romania, Venezuela, the United Kingdom, and, yes, even the United States. I have had numerous responses from women in New Mexico, California, Louisiana, Pennsylvania, New York, Kansas, and even Florida. But that's enough, for now I think you get the point.

As you can see, this method will get you any woman you want—maybe not a specific woman, but a woman of any age, any nationality, and better yet, a very beautiful woman you alone select. And no matter what age you are, you can use this information, apply these tools, and get a woman you can be proud of, one that you hand selected! I sent six hundred e-mails across the world to women ages eighteen through twenty-three. And I received more than 120 responses from women wanting to talk to me and learn more. I had to turn down the least attractive ladies and those whose personalities didn't exactly match what I was looking for. But after all, that's part of what helped me narrow down the search to just the right one.

Follow the advice in this book, and the e-mails will pour in and you will find the perfect woman. I will walk you through step by step, and you will be kicking yourself for not doing this sooner; if you had, you could be happy and with her right now.

Read on, my friend, and start a new life with the woman of your dreams. And remember: This book gives you the tools and knowledge to be successful in your search, but the final outcome will rest with you and your ability to get the woman to fall in love with you, or make her want to spend her time with you. So no more talk; let's start making this dream relationship a reality. The time to start is now, and I wish you the best of luck in your search!

Chapter 1

The Decision

First, you must decide what type of woman you want, including her physical and personality characteristics. Of course, many different types of women are available; your job is to pick those who will best suit you, in terms of morals and character as well as looks. You should also consider such things as accent, age, hair color, eye color, and even cultural background. This has to be something that you alone decide. Then, you are going to target these specific types of women, who can be easily searched for on any dating site found on the Internet.

Now, searching for women from other countries started many years ago, through so-called marriage agencies. But nothing was ever established to help men find women in the United States. The marriage agencies were mostly set up in Third World countries, because these women had no way to market themselves globally; they would hire these businesses to find them husbands by advertising in picture catalogs.

These small companies established a way for a man such as yourself to look for and pick a woman to meet or correspond with. They did not, however, set up dates or meetings when you decided to travel there. The businesses were just an avenue for women to list themselves; the agencies would run ads to get your attention, and when you contacted them they would send you a book of pictures for a fee. When you received this and looked through it, you could select the woman you wished to talk with. Did this mean she would respond to you? No! But you paid for the book; it wasn't the agency's problem if the woman didn't like you.

That's why this book is going to help you—because you select the women! And if they're interested they will contact you back, no money spent, no time wasted awaiting disappointment. An initial investment for the dating site fee for a month or so is all that you need, which works out to less than a dollar a day at most sites. Doesn't this sound like a cheap way to find a woman? It really is, and it works!

Marriage agencies worked very well in the past for getting a wife, but they are slowly diminishing because of the rapidity of the Internet, and the cost of seeking women online is significantly less. I have heard too many stories of men paying tens of thousands of dollars to get a bride through an agency; with my method, it could cost as little as twenty-four dollars and a plane ticket to go and see her. And with the women being more actively involved now than ever before thanks to the Internet, they are desperately trying to learn new languages. They are doing this now to further help them find a husband even faster, whether through their own initiative or because their parents are urging them to find a better and new way of life with a loving and caring husband (that's you).

This is your golden opportunity to make your life better, and theirs, too, in the process. So go ahead and decide now what you are looking for in a mate. In the next chapter we will discuss other qualities you may seek in the many available woman out there. Weighing their various advantages and disadvantages will enable you to decide on your wonderful new mate for life.

The nationalities of women that will be discussed have been chosen either because they are the easiest to get to come to the United States, or they retain all the core values and beliefs that existed so long ago, when marriage meant something stronger than it often does now in North America. Even so, your final choice can be of any nationality you may wish.

There are two countries in particular that I found still possess some of the traditional values most men search for but cannot find. After reading this chapter you must weigh each one before you make your final choice. You don't want to make a rash decision in this process, because this method involves a lot of time and you must be determined and committed in your quest. If you don't think first, and later you find your chosen woman can't come here for lack of a visa, then you just wasted valuable time and money setting up this dead-end relationship, and you've probably hurt or at least disappointed the woman. And let's not forget you're still alone!

We will touch base on some of the least targeted women; some good ones do exist in unexpected countries, but the time spent on these may prove to be fruitless. When starting your decision process, you should first check out the countries that I have listed for best possible candidates, because these women can be brought over to the United States without an entry visa.

Now, keep in mind that this list may change over time; you may need to see if there's an update available. But it's a good source of information for making your meeting easier; you don't have to leave your country, you merely bring her here to yours. And if you end up finding your woman in one of these primary countries and you develop something with her, the relationship will be much easier and the outcome will be faster. How, you ask? Well, for starters, you can fly her here with just a passport. She can live with you for up to the duration of the passport authorization, and develop your relationship. Then, if you're happy, you can apply for a fiancée visa and have her stay with you during the process. But don't forget she has to return to her home country once the visa is finally ready for her to get approval at the consulates.

But with this method you won't have to wait for her while you're filling out forms to get her here, and the process to get her a visa will be a lot easier. All in all the process will be a lot simpler and less expensive or time-consuming. Best of all, you won't have to be apart waiting for the government to approve a fiancée visa, a separation that is so common with overseas marriages.

Even if you decide to pick a different country and have the woman wait there while the paperwork creeps through the bureaucracy, don't let the long process scare you.

Now let's talk briefly about requirements for the countries that don't require a visa for entry into the United States. This information was taken from the Immigration and Naturalization Service Web site and is strictly for reference only. The information changes frequently, so you must check for updates.

Visas

Destination USA: Secure Borders, Open Doors (http://united statesvisas.gov) is an official source of information about U.S. visa policy and procedures.

Who must apply for a United States visa?

You must apply for a United States visa if you:

- have failed to comply with the conditions of any previous admission under the visa waiver program. This would include overstaying the period of stay granted on arrival, which may not be more than ninety days in any case, and may be less;
- intend to accept paid or unpaid employment in the USA (also applies to au-pairs and interns, working journalists, and government representatives on official business, among others);
- wish to travel to the United States for more than ninety days or in order to attend secondary school, vocational school, or university;
- have been denied entry on a previous occasion or have been expelled from the USA during the last five years;
- have a criminal record or suffer from a serious transmittable disease or mental disorder;
- are a drug addict or drug trafficker, or were involved in Nazi persecutions, and if you were or still are a member of a subversive or terrorist organization.

The United States Visa Waiver Program

The Visa Waiver Program (VWP) permits visa-free travel to the U.S., if you are a citizen of one of the following countries and conditions mentioned beneath apply to you:

Andorra*, Australia, Austria, Belgium*, Brunei*, Denmark, Finland, France, Germany, Iceland, Ireland, Italy, Japan, Liechtenstein*, Luxembourg, Monaco, New Zealand, the Netherlands, Norway, Portugal, San Marino, Singapore, Slovenia*, Spain, Sweden, Switzerland, or the United Kingdom. Citizens of Korea may not use the waiver, and must, therefore, obtain visas.

Note: Citizens of countries shown above with an * must apply for visas if they do not have machine-readable passports.

Note also: Cook Islanders holding machine-readable New Zealand passports are eligible to enter the United States under the visa waiver program, which allows for up to ninety days in the United States.

Uruguay has been removed from the list of countries participating in the VWP.

Guam Visa Waiver Program

There is a separate visa waiver program for Guam. Travelers from Guam Visa Waiver Program countries may enter Guam for business or pleasure and remain for up to fifteen days. Citizens of some countries, including Republic of Korea, may travel to Guam without a visa using the Guam Waiver Program. They must hold a valid passport and have a round-trip or onward ticket. No extension of stay, adjustment of status, or onward travel to another destination in the United States is permitted. Travel must also be aboard a signatory airline or ship.

People who are traveling to the United States or Guam for reasons other than business or pleasure exceeding ninety days (fifteen days for Guam) will need a visa. Also people who may be ineligible to participate in the waiver program because of certain medical problems, criminal convictions, narcotic addiction, or prior deportation from the United States will continue to need visas.

Citizens of the VWP countries can travel to Guam under the Visa Waiver Program.

For further information, see travel.state.goc/vwp.html and www.unitedstatesvisas.gov.

Conditions

You may travel visa free if you meet all of the following requirements:

- You are a citizen of one of the above-mentioned countries and hold a valid passport of that country. Please note that passports of certain countries need to be valid for at least six months prior to the date of departure from the U.S.
- You are traveling for business, pleasure, or transit only.
- Your intended stay in the U.S. does not exceed ninety days.

- You hold a valid round-trip, non-transferable airline ticket on an authorized carrier. Onward tickets may not end in Canada, Mexico, or the Caribbean.
- You will enter the U.S. aboard an air or sea carrier that has agreed to participate in the program. This applies to most airlines and shipping companies (private or official aircraft or vessels do not meet this requirement). You will need a visa if your carrier is not a participant.

However, please note that the following travelers will need a visa in any case:

- people who intend to work in the U.S. (paid or unpaid). This includes work as an au pair or intern, journalist, or government representative on official government business, among others;
- people who intend to stay in the U.S. for more than ninety days;
- people who intend to attend school or university in the U.S.;
- people who have been refused admission into, or have been deported from, the U.S. within the past five years;
- people who have been arrested or convicted for any offense or crime (including drug trafficking);
- people who have been afflicted with a serious communicable disease, or who are drug abusers or addicts;
- people who have participated in the persecution of any person under the control of the Nazi Government of Germany;
- people who have ever been a member or representative of a terrorist organization.

If any of the above applies to you, you are not eligible for the Visa Waiver Program and will need a visa to enter the United States.

If the country in which you are looking for your dream woman is not listed, then you will most probably have to go to that country to meet her, so be prepared. But also note that you will need a passport and a visa to gain entry, and each of the countries has specific guidelines to obtain them. A good site for visa requirements and costs listed by each country is http://www.pueblo.gsa.gov/cic_text/travel/foreign/foreignentryreqs.html.

Now, let me mention briefly two countries that have the most stunning and gorgeous women in the world: Ukraine and China. I have found them to be the ideal countries to search for a wife. Now, keep in mind that if you want a woman from one of these two countries, you will need to fly and see them; they cannot get a visa to see you. Maybe that's why they are in such a great abundance. I found through personal experience that the extra trouble involved in marrying them is well worth it.

Ukrainian women

Ukrainian women, as you will see during your search, display abundant beauty and poise. In my studies I have found that this country has the most beautiful women who are searching for a truly loving and caring man. Their ages range from eighteen to over fifty, and depending on what you're looking for they will make great wives. Although not all of them can speak fluent English, they do, however, want very much to learn. Most of them are very willing to leave their beloved homeland to be with a man who would love and care for them. Be aware, however, that just as in other countries, some of these women exploit your search as a means of income. This will be discussed in greater detail in the scam section.

The sizes and weights of the women here all vary tremendously, and you have your choice of qualities. A great number of these women attend college or already have degrees. They are also accustomed to making do with what they have and can survive with very little, if necessary. Their home life has been molded around traditional beliefs and values that will make them a very attractive prospect for any man. Many of them do not wish to live with, let alone to be married to, any of the men from their home country, as they can be abusive and do not necessarily think highly of women. They want to find a loving man to share their life and make a family with, and that man could be you.

Chinese women

Most Chinese women's body shapes and sizes follow the same pattern. Typically, Chinese women are petite, usually no taller then 5 foot 5 inches; of course, not all women of this country are short, but the majority of them are. You will find black hair and black eyes to be extremely common. Even their breast sizes appear to be generally modest, although if you looked hard enough you could find women who are tall or heavyset, or who have large breasts. Chinese women are also very clean and conscientious individuals, always keeping their appearance up. They typically remove all hair from their body and take baths before getting into bed at night, and even again first thing in the morning.

They have dreams of the future just as everyone else does, but their culture has been instilled in them from birth. They have been taught that the man is the head of the house and he makes all the decisions, and the woman is there to take care of him and love him and to spend her life with him making a family together. Their traditional values and beliefs make them most desirable and sought-after wives in today's society.

You will also find that families in China live together, sometimes two or three generations all under one roof, even sharing the same bed if the situation warrants it. They don't have the comforts we do here, and are used to lying on a wooden bed with no mattress; they live without even the simplest things that we have grown to expect from day to day. The woman in China are typically taught to cook at a very young age, and also are instructed in how to clean and how to be the driving force in taking care of the family.

Their food varies, but it consists mostly of seafood and vegetables. Although China has progressed through the years, most traditional dishes are still prepared in age-old ways. Even today most households use a wok as the main cooking utensil.

Most Chinese women who live in the city use either a bike or a moped as their form of transportation, and typically none of them have owned a vehicle, let alone know how to drive one. They venture out of the home to attend school or go to the market, but they can usually be found at home the remainder of the day. It seems that China is moving forward in today's society, but at a much slower pace than the rest of the world. They do have movies and bars and McDonald's, but not in great abundance, and a night out can cost a family valuable money they cannot afford to give up. This makes the women of this country seem very backward when brought into a country that has the advances and common everyday utilities that we have come to expect in the United States. But early experience doing without makes them perfect wives who can welcome and respect the things they are not able to have in China.

Here's some more of what I have learned about Chinese women, during conversations with many of them in various cities around the country. They all seem to share the same core values that so many of us search for and want. Although they have been oppressed by the men there, I found them to be very sincere in wanting a genuine and loving relationship. These women, no matter their age, are very dedicated to their husbands. Most who are single and never married are virgins, even well into their mid twenties. A loving and caring man will find a Chinese woman to be a jewel, something to treasure forever.

I have discussed only two countries so far, but I do not want to analyze every nation on earth. The women of every country have traits similar to those already mentioned, the emphases varying from one culture to another. But in my search I have found the women of Ukraine and China to be especially desirable to men looking for specific traditional values. Some other countries that share these same traits include the Philippines, with its great abundance of women looking to find a sincere mate, as well as Japan, Brazil, Venezuela, Norway, Sweden, Finland, and Romania.

Does this mean that countries I haven't mentioned should not be considered when looking for a wife? The answer to that is no, but you must look closer at who you are dealing with when you venture into these countries, and see if they in fact have the characteristics you're looking for. Some traditions and beliefs may not fit exactly what you want; you must research this closely to ensure that your desires are satisfied.

Does this mean that all the women of the above-mentioned countries will have all that you need? Of course not; great care must be taken when deciding on your target area, and the specific country you wish to find your wife in. But you must also remember that if you develop a relationship with a woman in any countries not mentioned on the visa waiver list, you will most probably have to go to them for a meeting. But we will discuss visas and travel arrangements in a later chapter. Your job, before you proceed, is to decide on a country and culture.

So, have you decided where you want to find the woman of your dreams? Let's see what you have so far: hair, age, color of hair, culture, country. Did you pick a country that requires a visa? Or did you decide on one that doesn't? This is just the groundwork for your search. When you have decided on all these things, only then are you ready for the next chapter, which involves a more precise breakdown of behavioral patterns and moral characteristics that you want and expect. When you have these basic things decided, move on: start getting closer to meeting and creating the relationship you so desire.

Chapter 2

Defining Your Ideal Woman

We need to spend some time now discussing the ideal woman you're looking for. This process is going to help you to not only define what you seek, but also help you in selecting or eliminating the women you talk with. Your job now is to think about what you want from this ideal mate, and what particular traits or character aspects you need, want, or even don't want in the relationship. I will get you started with some ideas to choose from, but I would suggest that you start your own list of what you want her to have. You can learn whether she possesses these elements as your correspondence with her continues. In order to make my own determination, I used a lot of different methods of communication that aid in this critiquing; I will discuss them in another chapter.

So let's talk about the main character traits you desire, the feelings and emotions you want her to have.

Get out a sheet of plain paper and start thinking of the different characteristics you look for immediately. When you've written them all down, circle the ones you feel very strongly that she must show or possess. Now, we both know you're not going to find the absolute perfect woman, as no one can be perfect—not even you— so pick the items on the list that you feel are the qualities absolutely necessary for you to be happy.

Here are a few ideas to get you started; and you should also think of some on your own.

Intelligent	Loyal	Hard-working
Beautiful	Trusting	Reliable
Moral	Loving	Energetic
Spiritual	Caring	Creative
Kind	Respectful	Knowledgeable
Traditional	Patient	Warm-hearted
Healthy	Humorous	Courteous
Vigorous	Happy	Curious
Inventive	Friendly	Ambitious
Enterprising	Determined	Artistic

So this is just one list of many things you can look for; I'm sure you have some elements of your own that I didn't mention. Use this list as an idea base to start your decision sheet.

Once you've done this, do the same thing with the characteristics you don't want from her. This may seem a bit strange because you may already know what you don't want, but you should make a list anyway as some of your requirements get clouded during your conversations and can get overlooked. Once you've compiled a list of qualities she must not have, if she does reveal any of them you'll immediately know she isn't the woman for you. Here are a few that I had down, just to start you off.

Thieving	Jealous	Overweight
Lying	Lazy	Uncaring
Alcoholic	Gold-digging	Argumentative
Two-faced	Mean	Distrusting
Hateful	Sly	Drug-addicted
Obscene	Perverted	Disrespectful

The information you just gathered will help you in so many ways; you will see how to learn the details of her personality when you get to the chapter that explains the various forms of communication you can use. These traits will come out during your conversations with her and help you eliminate many of the women you come into contact with. The traits you don't want are not easy to get from them, and, believe me, a lot of hard work and time are involved in this process. But now you know what to look for, and that makes the search easier; you are laying the groundwork to find a specific woman and you need all this information. Think of it as a road map to your final destination. You can drive around aimlessly, or you can have it all mapped out and save yourself precious time. I know when I was starting out I just went about it without knowing exactly what I was looking for. Sometimes this proved to be an advantage, because it forced me to continue to talk with my prospective ideal women. But most of the time I missed some qualities because I wasn't prepared, and realized only later that I'd been wasting my time.

I would even go a little further and say that we seem to live in an age of obsession with what's in style, and mimicry. What I mean is that I like to look for a woman who is not a follower, or doesn't do something simply because it's in style. You have some ideas now? Here in the United States, the big thing is eyebrow piercing, lip rings, or tattoos on the lower back—none of which I find attractive, and I knew these were definitely some of the things I did not want on my ideal woman. Defining your ideal woman is no easy task and it's one you must spend most of your time on; if you don't follow my advice and give it the right amount of thought, you will be upset at the outcome.

Defining your ideal woman envelopes the way she talks, her choice of words, the way she thinks and acts. You must consider all these things. I know this will seem like a small chapter on such an important topic, but I cannot get into great detail about something that you alone must think of and decide on. The different habits and traits she shows are basic things to examine and keep track of; but behavior and the way she thinks, acts, and feels are things that you must know and want. I'm not talking about different tastes in music or whether she likes to dance; these are small things that are not critical to true happiness. But there are certain things, positive and negative, you can write down on a piece of paper and look for, and most of the women you meet will fall into either your positive or negative category. As you talk and interact with them and see how they really are, they will slowly eliminate themselves. So take your time and think! Come up with the traits of the woman that you really long to be with; this will help you achieve your goal.

All finished? Now you have defined your ideal woman and are well on your way to success. Let's take our papers and set them aside as you start to read the next chapter and get started on making your profile and picking out the women you're interested in meeting.

Chapter 3

Choosing a Dating Site and Creating a Profile

So let us assume that now you're ready, that you have researched and found the ideal country and also the type of woman you want. Now comes the task of finding the appropriate Web site that has the kind of women's profiles you're looking for. Now, be aware that there are a literally thousands of sites available, and most of them will allow you to post your profile for free. But when you type in, say "dating sites" at an Internet search engine, you should examine different details to see that the listed sites have all you need. Remember, before you throw your hard-earned money at them, look at the sites closely. I want you to be successful at finding the woman of your dreams. So follow these guidelines when checking a site to join. Your goal is to find the woman whose qualities you listed in the last chapter, and she must be located here through this dating site; otherwise, you're wasting precious time and money.

Some questions to consider:

1. Will the site allow you to search the geographic locations before posting your profile to make sure your ideal woman can be found there?

2. Are there a good number of postings from the countries you have targeted to find a mate, to open up your choices?

3. How much does it cost if you want to sign up and send e-mails?

4. Do they have chat rooms, and also private chat rooms, so you may talk with your new friends once you have contacted them?

5. Will they alert you when someone has responded to your e-mail or has expressed an interest in contacting you?

6. Once a member, can you search for specifics like hair color, height, weight, and years of education?

You should try to find at least two sites that have all these capabilities; a great number do, but make sure they have the target geographical area and enough women for you to sift through and contact.

OK, now we're ready, right? We have the type of woman in mind, and we've checked out enough sites that we've been able to settle on two with plenty of profiles relevant to your requirements and that meet all the other criteria.

Let's begin now with making your profile. Most of the information is generic, like your age, weight, height, and whatnot, so this is no great task to enter. Soon, however, you will get to areas in the profile asking you such things as your interests and what you like to do in your spare time. You will also be able to specify what type of relationship you're looking for, and what characteristics you look for in a woman. Also, you can declare what type of man you are and what you want to emphasize to those women who read your profile, explaining exactly how you feel and what you are looking for in a relationship.

Now, be aware that this book is only a tool to help you find the woman you want as a companion and a wife. Although you can also use the guidelines in this book simply to meet and date, you must make sure you declare that intention if this is the case. The readers of your profile will be looking for the same things as you, and we don't want to misguide them into something they're not seeking.

OK, so you went to the site and created a user name and entered a password and all the basic information about yourself. Now let's discuss the type of person you are. Don't rush through this, as you have plenty of time to sit down and make a summary. You must do this for your profile to have the impact to get the most responses.

As you think about what you would like to enter at the site, take some sheets of paper and write down how you think the information about yourself should read. I would recommend that after each step is completed you type it into some word processing program so punctuation and spelling can be checked. This will also allow you to save the information for future uses; if you decide to start looking at another site, you merely copy and paste.

Introduce yourself with a "Hi" or "Hello" at the beginning, just as you would in the opening of a personal letter. Let the readers find out what you like to do in your spare time, including any activities you are involved in and any hobbies you may have. Don't forget to mention where you like to go in your free time.

You need to add some brief information that touches on aspects of your personality and what you bring into a relationship, and what special qualities you have that will make the readers want to respond to you. Here is an example of a profile that has proved to get dramatic results. Remember, this profile isn't necessarily you; use it only as an example to see how yours might be written.

Hi. I would like to tell you some things I like to do in my spare time. I love to go out on Friday and Saturday nights when I can in the summer and just cruise around in my sports car. I picked up the collector's edition Trans Am convertible; it's really nice. I like to show it off at car shows or just go for late-night drives. Other things I do in my spare time include just about anything from snow skiing to bowling. I don't care what it is, really; I just like to get out and have fun, although I also love to sit at home and cuddle up with my partner and watch movies.

I want to spend all of my free time with the woman of my dreams. "Who's this," did you ask? Well, I haven't exactly found her yet, but let's see if you might know her. The woman I'm searching for has to want a sincere, loyal, and trusting relationship that is very committed, and she wants it to last forever. A relationship where I would spoil her, and do all that I can to make her dreams come true. She's a woman who welcomes each day knowing that we are together, and this makes each and every day special. A woman who would appreciate roses for no occasion, or a gift just because, or even a night out with dancing and dinner that leads to a long walk holding hands.

I'm searching for a woman who wants everything in her life she has ever dreamed of to be made possible, and to love me the way I will love her. Do you know this woman? If so, send me a line and we can discuss it further. I know I would rather be enjoying each and every day holding you, and making these things happen right now. So come on—let's see if our destiny awaits. Let's seize this moment and spend our time with each other making wonderful memories.

(Source profile used by Sebastian Chance, 2004)

That's the profile I used to find my wife, and an example of what type of information I used to let her know how I thought and felt and what I was looking for. You can see that it touches on what this gentlemen likes to do in his spare time. It also speaks of what he wants to give in the relationship, and focuses on his priority being his partner, and makes it clear that he wants so much to find the right one; it even asks the readers if this is what they search for, too. You can add to or modify this in any way so that it becomes your own feelings and style, but try to keep to the general guidelines so that you can attract only the women you want to be with.

Now it's time for the meat and potatoes, shall we say. You have to create a description that will tell the woman who reads your profile what, exactly, you're looking for. Be specific; if there is something you must have from her, then write it down. But try to be realistic when you write it, as no woman—at least not that I'm aware of—will possess all the qualities you want. You should just try to touch on qualities that you feel you really want and need, as well as what you feel will make this relationship successful. I will again show you an example from the same profile I used before, which will give you an idea of how it should flow.

What I'm looking for is a woman who wants a real man who is sincere and caring, but yet someone who can fix and do anything. I've never failed at any task I ever went after, and I have always accomplished what I set out to do with great success. But the only thing I seem to have problems with is finding a woman who knows what she wants and is committed. It seems no matter how much I love her, or how much I do for her, and how wonderfully I treat her, I always end up getting hurt. Is there a woman out there who says, "Hey, I've had enough of being used and mistreated"?

There must be a woman out there who says, "I want someone who will love me unconditionally, not just for today but for the rest of my life. Someone who will put everything in his life second so that I may be happy! Someone who will talk with me and listen to me, someone who will make me laugh and be there in times of sorrow to comfort me. A man who will always think and feel that I'm the most important thing in his life, and be there for me forever. And when he says he loves me, it's forever."

Can you imagine a relationship built on a partnership, where every decision is discussed and agreed on? Where everything is 50-50 and each will help the other in our day-to-day responsibilities? Sounds wonderful, doesn't it? Too good to be true? But yet it is true, and if you're committed and searching for such a relationship, so am I. Contact me and let's get started on finding out how wonderful life can really be and what it's like to have someone who will be there and love you forever.

Now, as you can see, this did not say things like "You must cook and clean and wash my clothes." Even though these are things you may be looking for, you would have a hard time getting responses if you were demanding on any of these items. But most of those things are a given in today's day-to-day living, so you don't have to spell them out. Besides, the woman you are searching for and those who will respond to you will have most of these concepts in mind already. Also, as you talk with her, you will find out more of the things you need to know before making a final decision about her.

The idea here is to touch on how you think everyday life will go and how you and she will strive to make each day better than the day before. After all, you want to attract a woman, not send her running away! So once again, take your time and write these things down and try to compile something of how you feel and what she will have in the relationship, and how each of you will survive together.

So now we have your profile information; you have checked it and reread it several times, and you believe you are ready. Are you done? I should say not! Although you have the very base of your new profile, you must now compose an e-mail that you can send to your prospective lady that will make her want to contact you and learn more.

This introduction should not be very lengthy, but it must grab her and make her want to respond to you. She must think to herself, "I must talk with this man! For he has everything I'm looking for, and he feels very strongly about it, the same as I do." Again, I will show you a sample from my own correspondence that has worked to get women from eighteen to twenty-five years old, from all around the world, to respond to me. This method works really well, and I can assure you that it proved to be very successful in helping me finally meet the woman of my dreams. Here is the e-mail I was sending out to get the lady's attention; my success rate was almost half for all the woman I sent this to. Use this only as a guide to writing your own letter.

Let me take a moment to ask you this: Are you looking for a prince? By this I mean the man that you envisioned back when you used to read fairy tales. I just want to tell you that I strive to be exactly that. I'm looking for a woman who wants to be loved, cared for, listened to, and understood, and I'm looking for a woman who will give all these things back to me and more. I want to spend my life involved with her and being with her every day, enjoying our lives together. I want to make my life's goal only to make her happy and make all her dreams come true.

I have read your profile and I feel very strongly that we may have this magic, and if you like I would want to talk with you and see if this feeling is valid. Do you want these things?

If so, please e-mail me so we can start learning about each other, and move closer to having a wonderful life of love and happiness. I see this as a chance to do one of two things: either make a new and wonderful friend, or find the very much sought-after love and happiness that so many people search for but never find. I will fly you from anywhere, or retrieve you from the country you live in; I will do whatever it takes if you are the one to make all of our dreams come true. I will wait to hear from you and can only hope you want these same things as I do. Sebastian (Me@whatever-address.com)

Now, a few things to consider. This e-mail states what the man who sent it, in this case me, wants out of a relationship. It also makes the woman consider whether she would be happy with me. You can see that it also states that I want a happy life, a committed relationship, and my goals are a family and happiness. It also makes her think, as I question her a few times so she can either agree or disagree with what I am saying. Now, once she has decided I have shown my commitment to her, it also goes on to explain that I will bring her from anywhere in the world if necessary so that we can be together. This is very important, as these women typically have no means to travel to see you. And it also exhibits my determination to find a true love, and declares that I am willing to go to any length to be with her.

You must also make sure to include an e-mail address so that she can contact you; this will enable all the site members you contact, whether paying or not, to respond via your e-mail address. You see the whole key to your success is based upon the initial e-mail. This gets women to look at your profile, where they can really see what you're about. So this message must be composed properly, or you will fail from the start.

Once women read the e-mail and go to your profile, they can see all the information about you. And hopefully you have posted a picture so they can also view you. You do not necessarily need a picture, but I would strongly suggest it. Not only will it increase your responses, but it will show your sincerity. Let's discuss the picture. You must take some care when picking it out; don't just grab something from an all-nighter or some event where you didn't look your best. Does this mean a suit and tie? Of course not, but you should be prepared to have a very good picture that represents you at your best. I mean, after all, you're selling yourself! You wouldn't want to buy anything that was talked about so wonderfully and then when you saw it you found it to be not very pleasant to the eye. Just take the time, prepare, and wear something that is clean and neat. You can wear shorts and a tank top, whatever you want, but make them new and very appealing. Make sure you are clean and well shaven and, of course, you hair is combed just the way you like it.

The picture you post must be the best one you have. I would take several in various positions, and even recommend they be taken outside under normal lighting—on a boat, in a car, doing whatever you do. But look at each one and decide on the very best. Remember, this is what you will place in your wonderful profile. Spend some time and shave, get your hair cut or styled. I would always get mine colored; I liked to hide the gray so I would always look my best, and so should you. I would also take some time and go to a tanning salon, so I could have some color in my face and body. You see, this is very important: Above all, you just want them to write back to you. After that you will talk with them and win their hearts over to you.

OK, so now we're ready. It's about time, isn't it? Well, let's get started! Go to the Web site you have chosen, and pick a user name and password. Now, remember that the user name is sometimes, and almost always, the name on your listing, so you want something unique but nothing vulgar or obscene; you will definitely lose some respondents there without them even reading your profile. Once you decide on it you're in. If you're afraid you can't remember them, write down the user name and password, but the site will usually e-mail you the password if you misplace or forget it.

Start inputting your information just as you have written it down. If you saved it as I suggested you could open the file and copy and paste it in and save yourself some time. Once everything's done and all the information is set and ready, upload your picture to the Web site. Some sites have size limits, and if your photo is too big you can use a picture editor program to shrink it down. I use Microsoft Photo Editor, which works very nicely. I can also auto-balance the picture to change the lighting and make it more appealing.

Finally, your profile is complete and you're ready to go. Now, when you have finished entering all this, the dating site will review your profile and picture to make sure it meets with their standards. As long as you don't put your e-mail address or any personal contact information in there and the picture is not obscene, they should have it authorized within twenty-four to forty-eight hours and send you a confirmation saying it's been approved.

Now, read this entire book before contacting the women who respond. The next chapter will help you understand the forms of communication you can use, their benefits to you as well as their deficiencies.

Here we are. The profile's in and we're ready to start contacting beautiful women. You have the countries selected, and the women's age range. Then let's go!

The first time you try to contact a woman via e-mail, the dating site will have a pop-up that says you must upgrade to send the message. Now, some of them let you send a wink or some other signal free; this basically tells the woman you're interested. But this method has not proved to be very effective, and I don't recommend it. You want to send her that wonderful e-mail you composed; she needs to read this it and be won over. If the woman, even though she knows you like her and her personality, is not a member she cannot contact you, so you end up wasting your time. So go ahead and upgrade. But what I would do is find the smallest cost upgrade that will allow you to send e-mails for a month; don't spend loads of money and find out that this site hasn't produced any interested women. If you have set this profile up correctly you won't need it longer then a month; the e-mails to you will start coming in quickly and you will not be able to keep up.

In the initial search I always liked to go straight to the country of my choice, type in the age range, and see what women were posted there. Click on each one you find appealing and read her profile. When you decide on the one you would like to talk with, go into your saved e-mail and copy and paste your e-mail letter. Then send it to her. You can pick whatever you want for the subject line. I used either a HI or HEY to start it off. Now continue to do this until you have seen and sent all the e-mails you wish for each country.

Most sites will tell you the last time the woman visited. You should use this information to decide whether you want to e-mail her or not; it would not be very good to e-mail one who hasn't checked her e-mail box in a month, would it?

Are we done? Well, no. A proven technique I have discovered is something you should do at least once a week from now on. Log onto your dating site and check all the new profiles that have been added. You should do this at least every seven to ten days, always looking for more women to e-mail. Another method is to see who is online at the time you are; you should check on different days of the week and especially at different hours of the day. Why? Well, let's not forget that other countries are in different time zones. To catch different woman online, you must check during their local times. It reminded me of going out to fish at different times of the day; some hours are more productive than others. For instance, China is twelve hours different from Michigan; Ukraine is nine, Romania is seven, and the United Kingdom is five. I liked to go online at different intervals; by doing this I could catch women online, so their response time was faster. Doing it this way will give you the biggest bang for your buck. You can easily download a world clock and set up each country you want to monitor online. This will constantly update and keep you aware of the correct local time for the country you're targeting. They are typically available free, but more elaborate ones you can purchase very cheaply.

Responding to the new member profiles will have a similar effect, as new members will be checking in more frequently.

You must be very careful to make sure you know which women you have contacted already. I was able to remember most of them, although I did make a few mistakes and sent the same letter twice to the same woman. Not all of the sites I have found track whom you have contacted. So it will be up to you to make sure you don't write to the same woman twice; if this does happen, you can be sure she will lose all interest in you. She may even become very angry that you did such a thing. Also, never reveal that you are sending the same e-mail to several women; always make each one feel that she is unique and that you sent the message only to her. I made this mistake at least three times, but I was able to win the women back by explaining that the computer froze the last time I sent it to her and I wasn't sure she had received it, or that the webmaster is having difficulties with the e-mail system, sometimes sending a message up to three times to the same person. This worked for me but I really don't recommend trying it. Things can get a little nasty. If there are more women who interest you, just blow this mistake off and move on.

When the responses start coming you will need to read them all and think carefully about what you are saying when responding. You should put as much thought into this as you did your entire profile. During your conversations by any method, if you do things right she will want to hear from you again soon. Most of the women will respond to your personal e-mail box; some will give you their e-mail address as well. Be prepared for some to want to talk with you in real time and give you their phone number (which is rare, but does happen) or offer to chat with you on such programs as MSN Messenger, Yahoo or AIM. In a later chapter, I'll talk about how to get the best deal on phone cards when you get to the point of talking by phone. Right now, let's talk briefly about those three messenger services I just mentioned. These are online services that allow you to chat in real time. I would suggest that you log on now and make up a good handle (name) for yourself, as you may need to give it to your correspondents soon. You should take some time to familiarize yourself with each of these programs, if you haven't already, so you can see how they work, but all three of them are very similar. If you don't know about these or you have never used them, don't sweat it. I have a chapter just for you! More on that later.

At this point you have composed everything and your profile has been approved. Now you are searching for and contacting all the women you would love to talk with and possibly meet. Keep each response you get. I would check and see if it's possible at the dating site to make a personal folder; if so, create one and name it "received e-mails," and save it. This will enable you to track your progress and keep track of each responding lady's vital information, such as birth date, location, age, body type, and of course, picture.

At some point, I would even recommend creating a spread sheet to keep track of the name, country, state, address, age, birth date, and any other information you want to maintain for each contact. See below for an example of a sheet I developed. It is very easy to set up and will save you time when you want to send flowers or a gift.

NAME
COUNTRY
ADDRESS
AGE   BIRTHDAY
PHONE (HOME)   PHONE (CELL)

Now, as you can see, this is in very basic format; you don't need to be a computer whiz to make it, and you can modify it to suit your needs. Will you need to do this? Who knows? I did, though, and it helped me out a lot. You see, when trying to find the right woman, you must not just talk with only one woman at a time. You need to talk with several to be sure that you're not wasting your time on the wrong one, and ending up eliminating her later, and starting from scratch with the next. You will see this when you venture off into locations that are far away from you, and she proves not to be what you want. Why start all over again when you can just switch your attention to another woman you've already been talking with?

You'll find that some you talk with will eliminate themselves by getting distracted or even losing interest while contending with their everyday lives, so it will be necessary to set up a database to handle many women. For me it worked out great; I had more than eighty women at one time. I would drop a few and add a few as time went on, as I found some were not what I was looking for or they simply lost interest or weren't really sincere about what they were looking for. But using this method helped me keep track of very vital information, and when I wanted to send flowers or even money for whatever reason I had this information readily at my fingertips. Of course, this information will not be given to you right up front, but it will come over time, so you must make sure that you update the spreadsheet regularly.

When the e-mails start coming in you must make sure you keep the woman's attention. I like to tell her she's beautiful, or adorable, just talk with her like she's the only woman for me. I also address her with words like babydoll, sweetie, cutie pie, or something to that effect. Now, I don't use just a term like this once, but just enough to flatter her so she thinks I'm the greatest man alive. This has been a very powerful tool to use to establish a relationship with women. Most of these women have been hurt or cheated on and are looking for someone who can appreciate who they are and love them for that.

If you get onto instant messenger services, also remember this: It's best to keep them all blocked and only talk with who you want, one at a time. Take it from me—they will know if you take even a few extra seconds in responding that you're talking with someone else and not giving them all of your attention. All that hard work was paying off but then you blew it. Just talk awhile with her, and then find some reason to leave. Then you can start talking with another. Doesn't sound too difficult now, does it?

Just in case you need some more guidance, let's talk some more in the next chapter about your initial e-mail, as this is the most important step of the process.

Chapter 4

Your Initial E-mail

Now, remember, the women you're going to talk with are tired and very suspicious; a man, or perhaps several men, have hurt them in the past and they want someone sincere for a lasting relationship. They want a romantic, someone who tells them how beautiful and special they are, how smart and sexy. I have talked with many women and learned that if you want to win them over, you must prove to be something they have never encountered before. If you do this, you will melt their hearts and they will be yours. Every time I talk with any of them I'm always sweet and polite, but also I add some fun when I can. When you start talking with what may be the woman of your dreams, you will soon learn her personality and what is and is not acceptable to say. It's always awkward at first, but start off with a general goal, and ask questions like what she enjoys doing. Ask questions that will determine if you have something in common with her, try to build a friendship with her, and get some understanding of how her mind works.

Remember to take a second and think of your response; if you say something too fast, you could wind up blowing the whole thing. But when you talk make it seem that she has your full attention, and show her that you're very interested in her. Many of the buzzwords I have already mentioned work very well. If she says that things aren't going well for her today, respond with, "Aw, sweetie, what's wrong and how can I help?" If she complains about her features or how she looks and you have been talking with her awhile, say something like, "I wouldn't change anything about you. I think you're wonderful." Then pause for a second and say, "Well, maybe two things." It will drive her crazy, and of course she will ask what. And then you say, "Your last name and where you live." This will get them every time, and make them feel wonderful.

But of course this type of talk comes later, after some correspondence. When they send you pictures—and they will; if not, ask for them—make sure you do the same. Tell them how beautiful you think they are and how they are the most gorgeous women alive in your eyes. You must try and be romantic no matter what, and always keep this way of thinking; try to talk with them as if you're very much in love. Not all women will respond to this, but I have had so much more success when talking this way to them. You see, since they were small girls they have always been looking for someone truthful and honest, open and caring. But they also want someone who will involve them and listen to them.

Read their first e-mail back and make sure you answer all their questions. Then you can go on and say the rest in your own words. Here is my initial letter to them, but remember I always modified the beginning if necessary and then pasted the whole thing into my first response. And of course I always added to and modified it where necessary for each woman.

I work for [company] in [city, state]. My job there is [position], and I'm responsible for [specify tasks]. This has a lot of responsibility but I basically sit around during the week and respond to any breakdowns that occur during the shift and make a ridiculous sum of money for it (ha ha). I live in an apartment right now; it's a two- bedroom and the complex is new; in fact, it isn't fully completed yet. I will be buying a nice home someday when I meet the love of my life, so we can find it together. I go to the gym frequently, and always try to keep both my appearance and my body looking the best they can be, and yet I'm always striving for better. For fun I like to do just about anything, really. I have a sports car that I drive in the summer and take to auto shows, and during the winter I drive a Dodge Ram 4X4.

I also own a boat and love the water very much. I hope you do, too. I take the boat out on weekends and fish, tube, water ski, or just go out and enjoy the day. I also love amusement parks, especially the roller coasters. Also, I love to sightsee and sometimes run off on a whim and fly to just about anywhere to have a good time. But I also love to rent movies and just sit home on occasion and cuddle up on the couch for an evening. I'm attending college right now and have an associate's degree in electronics and four classes left for a business degree. After that, I will take online classes for my bachelor's. I love animals and although I don't have any yet, when I buy a house I plan on getting some pets. I also like to go horseback riding and do just about anything that has to do with being outdoors.

Well, I think you know some things about me now.

I will send some pictures of what I have been talking about and you should send some back also, as it helps to make things easier and gives you a better understanding of our conversation. If you have some more questions for me feel free to ask and I will answer any and all. Hope you're having a great day :)) Well, OK, cutie, I'll talk with you soon.

Sebastian

You see, this tells them so much about me for the first time: what I do for a living, where I live, what I drive, and it even gets into some personal things that I go even further into in my profile. These women are very fragile and will respond to any man who treats them well and talks to them with love and tenderness. That's what they are looking for, just a man who will love them and involve themselves and devote time to them. Opening doors and holding hands are just s few of the things they expect of you. With words you must do the same thing; you must make them feel you're with them, and when you talk with them it's like you're right there.

If you think of it like that, then you will say all the right things. I have talked in the same manner with some women that in no way would I ever want to be with, because their behaviors or thought processes didn't match mine. But I still treated them as ladies. I thought of this as a form of networking, and even though I don't match them, they are still new friends and they may have girlfriends who may be interested in me. You know, woman always love to match people up, so don't blow this chance. Who knows? You may be traveling there one day, and now at least you have a new friend to go and see. E-mail relationships are very hard and long to develop, but by following what I say you will succeed. Most relationships start off with first seeing and meeting a person, so there's immediate physical attraction. But you're doing the reverse, so you must make the best impression possible. No woman is impossible to win over; if you can talk with her as I have explained then it's possible for you to get her to develop feelings for you, and, yes, even fall in love with you, just through words alone and never meeting.

So take your time and think; be polite and romantic. Make her feel special in your eyes, and she will be yours! It won't matter what you look like after you meet. I mean, obviously the pictures you send must be yours. But if you apply everything I have told you, once you communicate with her and use the endearments and style I have suggested, she will fall in love with you. Not the picture of you, but your personality. I have been able to be a boyfriend to many women, and, yes, I have even become engaged without meeting the woman face-to-face. Were they all out of the country? No, some were even in the U.S. and Canada. Apply my ideas, and if they contact you, use your new skills and your personality to make their minds and hearts scream your name.

Chapter 5

Win Her and Her Heart

Now we're going to recap everything you have learned so far. First, you have decided on everything you're looking for in your ideal woman. I made you think of all the physical characteristics you want her to have, and you have compiled a list of certain traits and beliefs you feel she must possess, as well as some of the characteristics you don't want her to have. I have discussed different countries and the advantages and disadvantages of searching for a woman there. You developed your profile and you have it posted in at least two sites, and you're actively sending out e-mails to women you're interested in to make them want to contact you.

Now the e-mails are coming in, and your next question to me is, "What's my next step? What do I say now that she has contacted me?" We're going to touch on some of the things you need to do as you filter through your discussions with her and decide if she's the right woman for you. Earlier I talked about how you should always talk politely with her, and also come across as being happy. And I even gave you a few endearments to call her by, right? But these alone cannot win her over. You must work at this, and gain her trust. This process can take from a few weeks to even a month or two. Now, don't get discouraged. You chose this method, and why? Because it works! But you have to spend some time if you really want to succeed.

When you start your first conversations with her, they can be by e-mail, messenger services, or, if she's aggressive enough, a phone call, but it is very rare for her to give out her number so early in the game. When you start to talk with her, it's like a learning stage. You have to watch everything you say; you can easily offend her, so make sure you're very polite and just ask uninvasive questions about her, like where she works or whether she goes to school, maybe what she likes to do on the weekend for fun. Your goal here is just to try to find out a few things about her. Don't be pushy and start asking her out or coming on too strong; she don't know you, and most women are leery about stalkers or may assume that you're just another guy trying to score with her.

So ask her these things gently; you'll know how the conversation's going as you talk. But make sure you don't swear or say something out of line; at this point in the relationship it's vital to remain calm and just become friends.

So when I'm talking to her my initial words may be "Hi, beautiful" and then "How's your day going?" or "How was your weekend?" She is already going to be flattered just because of my opening statement. Trust me: It will also help her to relax. Now her response hopefully will be, "Good, and yours?" So you explain to her how your day has been, but don't start complaining and using her for a sounding board. Whether your day was bad or not is irrelevant. Your response is, "Very good, thank you, but it's much better now that I've had the chance to speak with you." You see, you're laying the groundwork, so to speak; you want her to have the very best conversations with you from the beginning, so she'll want to speak with you more. Your conversation should always make her smile and also feel special in your eyes; after all, that's the way you want her to feel. As the conversation continues on and she says things about what she does, or would like to do. Make sure you show her you're interested in any and all of what she does! If she says, "I play the piano," your response should be, "I love the piano and I've always wanted to play." And you might add, "It takes a very musically inclined person to manipulate both hands, I mean just doing so many different things at one time. I'm very impressed. I never could manage that." Of course, she will answer that you could do it and she even might offer to show you how. Are you starting to understand now? You already opened a chance to go and meet her!

Here's a small part of a conversation where I won over an eighteen-year-old girl within a week. Yes, you can do it, too! It's really not that difficult, but you have to be smooth and watch what you're saying. I told you before: You want to be unlike anyone she has ever met before.

Me (2:30:42 PM): You're adorable
Her (2:30:49 PM): am I really?
Me (2:30:59 PM): yes I think you're a very special woman
Me (2:31:03 PM): why you ask me
Me (2:31:08 PM): I told u you were
Me (2:31:09 PM): hehe
Her (2:31:24 PM): hehe thank you I think you are very good-looking
Me (2:31:34 PM): Thank you baby
Me (2:31:46 PM): but I must admit I think you're also very beautiful
Her (2:32:09 PM): hehe thank you so what kind of trips do you take?
Me (2:32:20 PM): really anything baby
Me (2:32:31 PM): like I'm going to cedar point this month
Me (2:32:35 PM): no biggie
Me (2:32:44 PM): but also on labor day I'm going to Texas
Me (2:32:53 PM) I like to travel and I want to go to Edmonton in Sept. also
Me (2:33:07 PM): they have the biggest mall in the world there
Her (2:33:16 PM): I love malls
Me (2:33:21 PM): no way
Me (2:33:27 PM): I love walking hand in hand
Me (2:33:40 PM): and watching u try on clothes and model for me
Me (2:33:41 PM): hehe
Me (2:33:49 PM): and of course u can buy whatever u want
Me (2:33:51 PM): lol
Her (2:33:56 PM): hehe whatever I want?
Me (2:34:03 PM): of course I dont care
Me (2:34:12 PM): its my job to spoil u crazy
Me (2:34:13 PM): haha
Her (2:34:24 PM): hehe wow i like soo how old are you?
Me (2:34:36 PM): I thought I told u haha
Me (2:34:38 PM): 38
Her (2:34:50 PM): thats cool not too bad
Me (2:35:13 PM): aw thanku cutie

Can you see what I mean from this conversation? I just met her, and she's only eighteen, but I sparked an interest in her and then flattered her even more, and after I laid the groundwork she came out and asked me my age. Of course I trimmed two years off of it, but hey! Thirty-eight sounds much better then forty, right? I mean, even thirty-nine would sound better. It's the initial sound of it that scares them. But you can see that when she asked me it was already too late; I already started to win her over. Now, not all women are this way, but a lot I have talked with are.

Let's go back to the little age thing, shall we? That's why advertising does so well; haven't you ever heard of something selling for just $19.99? That's because even though there's just a one-penny difference, $19.99 sounds a lot lower than $20; it plays with people's heads. Now, I'm not telling you what to say or suggesting that you lie. Say whatever you want. But for me, I wanted to make this relationship work, and I can deal with the age discrepancy later on if the relationship works out. I mean, come on, it's only two years! Once she develops feelings for you, even twenty years won't matter, although this great an age difference is not recommended and you shouldn't even think of it. The object is to make her like you, and if you say the wrong thing or don't market yourself right, you'd better just pick yourself up, dust yourself off, and get ready to start all over again. We're not talking assets or income or anything like that; it's a little hard to meet her in a 1988 Dodge Caravan when you told her you drove a Jaguar. So be honest about the rest of it; if you don't, you will find after spending all this time and finally meeting this wonderful woman she'll end up hating you just because you're such a liar. But shaving two years off your age? You can say, "I did it because I was afraid if I said forty I would lose you and I just thought you were the most wonderful woman I had ever met and couldn't risk that." This she can forgive! Saying you make $120,000 a year when you only make $40,000, she may have a problem with. But the two-year age thing she'll never ask about, and if she does you'll already have her in love with you and she won't care about such a small thing.

If you're worried that your salary isn't impressive enough, listen to me: You said you wanted a real woman, one you will love and who will love you forever. The money won't matter to her; just to be with you and be happy, that's what our goal is and this is all she wants.

During your discussions, if you can add humor to the conversation this will help, too. When you find the chance to get some humor out of the situation then you should try and do so, but make real sure it's acceptable to her. What if she will think your supposedly funny comment is out of line? If you have to think about whether it is or not, then don't say it. Otherwise, humor is the best medicine and can make her love you even faster. All women love to be with a man who makes them smile and can show them a good time. I know you're saying, "But I'm not funny." Who is? You're just taking a normal situation and making it seem funny! Most of the time she will say something that will open up the chance for you to make her laugh, and you have to seize this opportunity.

I have talked with more women than you probably have in your whole life, and it's always the same. They are looking for the perfect man. No, not one who is flawless. One who will listen to them, talk with them, someone who will make them feel special and loved. Sure, money and fame are great, but that's not what they're after. From their very first relationship these women have found out that most men aren't ready for a one-woman commitment; they just want say whatever it takes to get in their pants. Yes, this will make your task harder, and it will be difficult to convince them you're not like that. But you will be able to do it, as you speak with what may be the woman of your dreams and compliment her, just as I explained in my earlier chapters. Show her you are not what she is used to. The very first words I always use are "baby" and "sweetie"; talking like this will never make her mad at you. But this doesn't mean you can get real forward; just use nice, cute names that will make her smile and feel special and let her know you like her.

As your conversations progress you will learn much about her, even many things she has never shared with another person before. If you can sympathize with her, or share an experience of yours similar to one she has had, this will help to strengthen the bond between you. Maybe you can tell her of a similar thing that happened to you, and then both of you will get a laugh out of it, or at least share a mutual understanding.

This period during your initial conversation is crucial; you want to keep the conversation going, and always remember to let her be the one to have to end the conversation. If at all possible, talk with her until she has to leave; it helps to end the conversation on a softer note if she does it first. The result will be her getting back on later and wanting to talk with you again; in fact, she will be out there looking for you specifically if you've done this right.

Did you notice in the sample conversation earlier that I talked about the things I wanted to do, and the places I was going? Yes, it's early, but I'm creating interest in her to want to go with me. Even if the event is later down the road, just making her aware of it and the fact that you're going alone will make her think. Then, if it's possible, you can bring it up a week or two before it happens and ask her what she's doing, and if she would like to go. You know, even when I talked with women in all different countries, I still told them of my plans. I just changed it to say how wonderful it would be if she were able to accompany me on this trip or event; I know we would have such a great time together and wish there were some way it could come true and we could be together. I would even offer to fly them here for the weekend so we could go together, or I would talk about my going there and spending the weekend doing anything she would like to do. My whole goal was to make her want to see me, be with me; this brings closeness to the relationship and gives you a chance to meet with the real woman.

Here's an example. I talked with a young woman from Arizona for months; she came back later and finally said how nice it would be for me to fly there and share the weekend with her, going for walks, seeing a movie. But when it came time for me to set up the trip to be with her, this is what happened. I checked the flights and made sure my schedule was open. This is very, very important: Make sure she has agreed on all the details before you buy the tickets! Once I found out the flight times, I called to check that she would agreed on them. Everything appeared to be all right, but then I asked her what kind of car I should rent, as I wanted to keep her involved and also wanted to get something that she would like. Her response back to me was, "You're really coming here?" I said, "Yes, don't you remember? You asked me to come and see you!" Then she came up with an excuse that her mother was coming over Sunday and this and that was going on. I said to her, "OK, wait a minute. You asked me to come there." She said "Yes, but I didn't realize I'm going to have things to do." I then decided it wasn't going to work out with this woman and ended it there.

So you can see, even after months of talking with her and discussing it, she was still scared of actually meeting me. That's what the real problem was, and if all my wonderful talking and months of work hadn't convinced her of my trust and sincerity, then nothing ever would. Don't let this discourage you, but now you can see why I was juggling up to eighty women at one time. You can see how they may drop out even after a few months, so don't focus everything on just one. Your whole goal here is to talk with her, make her like you and trust you, and finally want to see you. Most women are scared to come to a place where they have never been if they have never met you. So you must go to the woman yourself. After all, your objective is to share some time with her and make her see you're a wonderful man and understand that she needs you in her life each and every day.

Now, remember, even though I have given you these pointers on how to act and all the things to say to her, it's always going to be up to you. I recommend that until later, when she starts the conversation off, don't talk to her about sex or your past love experiences; don't offer her any information about anything she doesn't come out and ask for. Then when she does, watch what you say and always, when it comes to love and heartbreak, make it clear that you are always the one who has been hurt. You gave all that you had and loved like no other man ever could, and yet it still wasn't enough for your ex-girlfriend. You're just a man in search of a true and loving woman who wants to have a committed relationship in which the rest of your life will be spent loving each other and sharing your lives. With you making her feel like she's the only woman alive, and telling her how beautiful and smart she is, you are well on your way to making a strong relationship of trust and understanding. You need to do this, as every great relationship must start off with these things and you must first and foremost become great friends with her; only then can you build this new relationship. She will soon be thinking of nothing but you, and I also believe you will think of nothing but her.

I've found through my conversations that, yes, good physical appearance is always a big plus in a relationship. And of course even age may be an issue when it's all said and done. But when you start to work on her mind, you are tapping into her true feelings. By merely talking with her and sharing things, getting her to listen and hear how you are and the way your mind works, this puts such a

strong hold on her that later, looks, age, or income will be insignif-
icant and overlooked.

There's not very much more I can say to you now on this topic.
It's a pursuit that you must endure alone; you must make her yours
with all that you have. I can't sit here and write every conversation-
al item that may come up; you must take on this task and get her to
love you. But use the tools you have just read about, and with your
own words and by applying these critical elements, you will come
to think this way normally. Then you will prevail. The whole key
here is you, and the biggest thing you have going for you is that she
wants these things said to her, she wants to meet the man you have
made yourself out to be.

When you do get to meet her, be the same man. Talk the same
talk. You already have her, but seal it when you meet in person. She
will always want to be with you. I hope this will help you with your
correspondence with her, and I assure you it has worked time and
time again with me. Just apply these ideas with your own personality, and she will fall in love with you, even by means of a computer and never meeting. My advice is the greatest help to you in your
search and will enable you to win over any woman.

Flowers and gifts

So you would like to send something to your woman; it's really
not that difficult. And as I recommend elsewhere, this is the simplest method of verifying that a woman is being truthful and actually exists. So why not send some flowers? It's the best method I
have seen.

I first made the mistake of thinking that I would use the same
service as I do here in the U.S. Not a good idea. First off, you can be
sure they will have limited items you can send, and the arrival time
will not be consistent. Also, you can get the currency exchange for
the destination country by purchasing the flowers in your
ladyfriend's country using that currency, but obviously to do any of
this you have to have a credit or debit card.

If you search on the Internet for flower vendors in her country,
you can be sure of finding someone local, and they will usually
deliver the next day. This is nice because of the time differences
between here and there. I went to send flowers to China when it
was 7 p.m. here. Well, there's a twelve-hour difference in China, so

when I placed the order it was effectively delivered within hours of my call. Also, you can take advantage of the exchange rate and if you pay in U.S. dollars you can save money with the conversion. Many people will try as I did at first and lose money if they don't order flowers abroad. But don't worry about that! Let your charge card work for you and the bank can exchange the currency for you at the current market rate.

This will also work very nicely with gifts. But I would recommend something small and not very costly at first until you verify her address and know that when you send something she will get it. I mean, even if she tells you her correct address, that doesn't mean she will get the gift, as these countries have an abundance of postal theft. So be smart. If you want to get her something expensive, say over $100, then I would spend a few dollars more and have it sent through a carrier like FedEx or some other private company that doesn't deal with the foreign postal service.

All right. I have discussed the content of the initial correspondence with you; now let's look into more detail on the technical aspects of communicating via the Internet.

Chapter 6

Forms of Electronic Communications

There are five different forms of communication that you can use to find and meet your dream woman on the Internet, and each one will help you to discover if she has the qualities and behaviors you're looking for:

- e-mail
- instant messenger services
- phone calls
- Web cams
- photos

Of course, when the conversation first starts out, people will always act differently than they would normally. It's awkward when you start to communicate with someone and try to know if she is acting this way or if this is how she normally is. That is why many of these interactions will be needed before you can detect the true person. Most people don't act differently intentionally; it's just a form of shyness or fear of rejection that keeps their true personality locked up, and through correspondence and using each one of these communication methods you will be able to bring this out. But over the course of time, and it will take you some time, each of you will become more comfortable with the other. This is where you really get to know who it is you're talking with. Let's start by discussing each form of Internet communication and see what each one has to offer when you're trying to find the true person behind her mask.

E-mail

It is very hard to picture or learn about a person strictly through e-mail. At this stage you haven't even met her, and of course things are going to be said in each message in such a way that of course it's what you want to hear. Does this mean she's being false or misleading you? Of course not. What it means, however, is that both you and your correspondent have time to think out each and every sentence you say to each other, and this allows for some smoothing over of true thoughts. So the best thing you can do with e-mail is to find out her interests or what goals she may have—information such as likes and dislikes, what she wants to do with her life, her favorite foods, and the types of music she listens to. In this way you can learn truths about that are believable. You can also ask questions about her beliefs and how and what she wants from a relationship. But questions like these will not be very personalized, and each woman will probably respond to you in the same way, that she wants a caring man who will love her and be true. But you can also ask specific questions, like if she enjoys roller coasters or if she would fly in a plane. These are things you can use to determine your compatibility with her.

Here's an example of an exchange I had with a woman. During our conversation by e-mail I had told her that I owned a boat and asked her about her thoughts about the water. I also talked with her about coming and seeing me in my state and asked if she would consider flying to me if I paid for the flight. In her response I found out she didn't like boats and was afraid of the water; she was also very afraid to fly or even ride roller coasters. Now, even though I still considered her a friend, I eliminated her from my possible matches. True, she was very young and beautiful, but this didn't sway my decision, and by using this method of communication I eliminated her as a possible woman of my dreams.

You, too, must use this type of screening to make these determinations. When you start off with e-mails, ask specific questions that will elicit very truthful explanations of how she thinks and feels about specific issues. If you can find things in common with her during your e-mail exchanges, then she is ready to progress to the next level of the relationship.

Instant messenger services

I find this form of communication to be the best to determine the true nature of the person you're talking with. I have had a lot of luck eliminating many women with this. Messenger communication is a one-to-one form of talking. Although you still have time to think about what you're saying, the time span between comments is short and it helps you to make the experience more personalized.

Also, it enables you to feel her every word while she can feel yours; this creates emotions between the two of you. it's a form of communication that alerts more of your emotions as it becomes more interactive. Furthermore, the messenger services usually have icons, or smileys as their called, which can be used also to liven up the conversation and show how you're feeling at that moment. This form of communicating gets both of you involved. I check for many things when talking with a woman by this method. I look to see when she is online; if she is really interested in you and something meaningful is developing, then she will be online looking for you to talk to and be with every day. An instant messenger experience I had with one woman helped me eliminate her from my list. I will give you the scenario.

She was very beautiful and young and she had a wonderful personality. Our conversations grew to be very long and enjoyable. When I talked with her we laughed and made each other feel many emotions, and always found ourselves smiling and having a great time. But there were some things she would do that troubled me. I never knew when she would be online; it varied all the time and I found myself always waiting for her. Even though I asked her about it, the behavior never changed. Now I know that we live different lives and both of us had things going on and we couldn't always talk at the same time. But my problem was this: She sometimes would not be online at all, and it might be days before I could talk with her again. Also, sometimes when we talked—and this happened very frequently—she would say she needed to go and do something and she would be right back. Now, granted, things come up and we have to leave and cannot talk, but I found myself waiting hours for her to return. Sometimes she said she would be right back but never came back online that whole night.

Now, to me this showed that she did not have her mind made up that I was the man for her, or at least I wasn't important enough for her to come back and tell me that something had come up and she wouldn't be able to talk with me. So even though she had many qualities that I searched for in a woman, you can see that she was-n't dedicated and wasn't thinking of my feelings. This is also true with several of the women I've met face-to-face. Many women out there are looking for the same thing as you. But you will find that some of them—but not all—lack the drive to move things forward and keep the relationship alive. By this I mean they start off with good intentions but then they lose interest in you, or the thought of going online to talk with you becomes secondary to them. This is a very good thing to find out before you spend a lot of time trying to build a relationship with a woman. Now, with this young lady I just used as an example, I had spent three months before this started happening, so it's not always apparent at first. But I knew that if she loved me and wanted to spend her life with me, she would put forth more effort in trying to get online and talk with me.

Now let's look at another young woman I started talking with by instant messenger. We found we had so much in common. I tried to get online at the same time each day, and if not we would work out a specific time so we could talk. This woman was always there waiting for me; each day like clockwork she would be there online. We talked for hours, and I could see her devotion and how much she cared. One time I was talking with her I had to run out for a few minutes and I told her I didn't know how long it would be. She understood and told me to go, and she would check and see if I had returned later. What I found when I came back some forty minutes or so later was her still there, sitting and waiting for me to return, because she wanted to talk with me so badly. "This is what you're looking for," I thought. Not only does she show she loves me, but she's willing to wait even forty minutes just to have the chance to chat.

So you can use this method of communication to pull out most of her personality traits, and lay the groundwork for seeing what she's really like and how dedicated she is to the relationship. And I strongly recommend this form of communication if possible after you have corresponded with e-mail or even at the beginning of your relationship. Be aware that some women do not have comput-ers or even access to one that can be used for instant messaging, or because of language barriers they cannot use instant messaging successfully. It's a tool that can help you; you do not necessarily have to use it, but if it is available I strongly recommend it.

Now let's talk about some of the don'ts of using instant messaging. When you have several women on your list, you need to do one of two things. Either block all of them and talk with them one at a time, or use invisible or away mode. Why is that? Well, if you have them all on and not blocked, then when you log in they all know you're on and will start to talk to you all at once. This can get confusing and you won't be able to keep up with all of them. You want to lose a relationship with a woman? Try taking too long to respond to her! She knows you're either talking with another woman or you're doing something else and ignoring her. Give her your full attention. Also, you might say something to one that you intended to say to another.

Here's another don't: You're talking with a woman and another sends you a message that you're not prepared for. Too many times when I was writing to one woman the cursor moved to the new box, I didn't know this, and I finished what I was saying and hit send and half the line went to the other woman! Have fun explaining that one! You may as well consider this young lady gone from further correspondence. Trust me; play it safe and never let them know you're online unless you initiate the conversation. You can always come up with something pressing to do later and tell her you have to go. Then block her and start talking with another one. I also made it a practice to never call any woman by her name, only by some cute names I gave her. And if you give them all the same names you'll never have any issues with calling them the wrong one.

With each one of the messenger services you can define a group and add e-mail address or whatever names your correspondents are using for that messenger service. What I did to help myself out was this. Suppose I just met a woman and through talking with her I knew her name was Mimi, and she lived in Montana and she was twenty years old. So what I would do is make a group called Mimi 20 Montana. Then I would add her sign-on name; this is the name she chose when she signed up for the messenger service. So now each time she got online, I knew immediately who she was and how old and where she lived. This helped stop some of the "I don't know" responses from happening. Believe me, sometimes during the conversation one of these three things is certain to come up and now you're prepared.

And remember, never, ever use their real names! I cannot stress this enough. Are you going to remember them all? Call them by pet names. I have told you a few; here are some more: babydoll, sweetie, cutie pies, pork chop, dumplin, sweet cheeks. I'm sure you have some of your own; get them into your vocabulary and use them all with each of your correspondents. You will never make a mistake by calling one woman something that you call them all by.

I'll explain more about instant messaging in the next chapter.

Phone calls

This form of communication obviously can make or break a relationship. It's no different from standing in front of them and talking, and you can seriously hurt a relationship with your mouth. You can hear her voice and any emotions she may have, but she can also hear yours. Phone calling is very personalized and you can start to detect even more of what she feels and thinks. I find it creates a better atmosphere between the two of you and really helps to build the bond between you and strengthen any emotions each of you may have. But keep in mind it also brings out the bad things; many phone conversations I have had have helped me to determine if this was the woman I was searching for or not. Now there are a lot of complications with this method, such as language barriers and the availability to call each other. On several attempts to call abroad I was not able to get through. But these problems can be easily overcome if you put forth some effort. Most of the women I talked with could speak some English and talk back with me, but still I have had some difficult conversations.

What I found out is that you must slow down when you talk, give her some time to understand you and listen to what you're saying. If you do this then chances are she may be able to interpret and process your words, although you may find yourself repeating the same statement many times during your conversation. But don't get upset, and try to understand that this form of communicating is difficult for her, but she is trying to talk with you and become even closer. Sure, it would be nice to just call anywhere in the world and talk in your own language and have no problems, but if your thinking follows this line then I would suggest you make sure you put this in your profile or use it as a guideline in your selection of possible candidates. Remember, though, that the more selection specifics you make, the more you are limiting your search for your ideal woman.

And make absolutely sure before you call her that you check in a later chapter on how you can keep money in your wallet when making calls overseas, so she doesn't become a financial burden to you.

Some advice on phone cards

So you're working it pretty well, and you both seem to have a lot in common. She gives you her phone number; if this is out of the country, you can expect it to be on the order of twelve numbers. Here's how the number is broken down First, the country code. For the entire U.S. this is the 1 at the start of the number, then the area code followed by the actual phone number. In other countries it's similar, except the country code is followed by what is often called a city code, rather than an area code. The country code for Venezuela, for instance, is 58. Then the city code let's say 212, means you're calling Caracas. Then comes the actual phone number, which looks similar to ours. And let's not forget that from the U.S. you have to start with the international dialing code of 011. So the complete number for a call to Caracas, Venezuela will look like this: 011-58-212-123-4567.

Seems long, but this is how it works. Now you can see how the spreadsheet works wonders for keeping track of them, although I also programmed them in my cell phone just for added convenience. But do not call from your cell phone, as the cost is enormous; the call from a cell phone to Venezuela costs sixty cents a minute. When you're ready to call her, go online and search out calling cards. There are literally hundreds of places to get them. What I did was find one that enabled me to pick the country I was calling. Select your card based on that as well as cost per minute and connection ranking; each card should show you how it are rated for connection and dependability. Also, see if it has any maintenance fees or connection fees; avoid these if possible. I bought a $10 phone card one time and during our conversation I lost the connection four times. It cost me to reconnect each time, and by the time I was done I turned two hours of available time to fifteen minutes through these charges.

There are many cards for each country so shop around; if you can find one that has at least four to five stars of reputability and a small maintenance fee and no connection cost, chances are this is a good deal. Cards are offered in different denominations, but $5 and $10 cards seem most common. How my system worked was like this: I selected how many cards I wanted and then paid for them. Then I'd receive an e-mail with an 800 number so I could call from a landline or cell phone. But be aware that your cell carrier may still charge your peak minutes for the call depending on the carrier and plan you have, so check out their policy on 800 numbers. The calling card e-mail also listed the authorization code for each card. So I would dial the 800 number and then enter the authorization code and then the phone number, and I was talking with her for just pennies a minute. Now, be aware that some calls won't always go through and you may have issues with noise or whatnot, but you will find it works well for what you need. Also, the site I used offered a 5-percent reduction on their prices if I spent $20 and a 10-percent reduction if I spent $40, so that was a nice little bonus. I'm sure you're saying, "What is this site?!" So I will tell you. But will it be the best site for you? You need to determine that for yourself, but I found it suited my needs and I could use the card for many different countries, and the cost was cheaper on a landline. For instance, if I called one young lady in England on her landline it was two cents a minute, but to call her on a cell number it went to twenty-nine cents a minute. I doubt you will ever find a cell number cheaper. All right, now here is the site: www.callingcardplus.com. You should find this helpful, but shop around if you want to find something better.

Web cams

This to me is the absolute best way to meet the woman you've been talking with, and really get to know her. You can use this device with any of the instant messenger services, but I found MSN to be the best with updating the image, making her image seem life-like and in real time. I also used Yahoo, but found the image update was not as fast and made you look more like a robot; still, this works very well if you have no alternative. If you're lucky enough she may already own a Web cam and you won't have to ask her to purchase one or turn it on, but before asking about this you should make sure you get one for yourself. They are found in just about any computer store or you can order them online, and they range in price from $20 to more than $100. I purchased a mid-priced one and found it to work very well for my needs; there's no reason to spend a lot of money for one that follows you as you move. Check your budget and buy one that won't leave you broke, but provides a clear picture. This is probably the most interactive device you can use; it enables you to fully meet the woman without actually being there.

Now, be aware of two complications with the cams. They flip your image as if you were looking in a mirror; you can't really tell until you watch your own motions. It's not a big problem; I just wanted to make you aware of it. Another thing is that you can't really see small things on the image of the other person, such as little scars or pimples. Even lighting changes her complexion. Lighting is a key issue with these; a small light behind you or off to the side is best.

Now back to your conversations with the women. Of course you can use the messenger box and type your words as usual. But if you have already called her, then you can talk on the phone and see each other using the cam; this gives you the feeling of being there and really helps develop a relationship. What I liked about this device is you can see the reaction to your conversation, and she can see you smile or frown, and see exactly how you react to her words. But beware that whatever is going on behind you is apparent to the viewer. So make very sure that what is taking place in the background is something you would want her to see or know about. You must always remember that everything you do is being watched. But at least the cam will let you know it's on; you see when you open the window what she is viewing. So you know it's working and it takes a few seconds to start, so you have time to turn it back off if necessary. The messenger will also ask you if you want to accept the request to show your image, so you can keep the cam from ever being activated.

I talked with many women through this method, and it makes the relationship so much better because you can see exactly who it is you're talking with. If you're at the point at which you're serious about the woman, try to get her a cam. But this only applies if she has access to a computer and can install one. Most women, if they are sincere and have developed a relationship with you, will buy one. But remember that most of the ladies from overseas don't have a computer, and they use an interpreter to talk with you through e-mails, so they probably cannot access a cam. But don't let this barrier stop your relationship, unless of course you make this a priority before meeting with her personally.

Here's an instance where I was talking with a woman and I felt she was exactly what I wanted. During our conversations she told me it was her birthday; of course I asked her how old she was and she said twenty-two. Then I asked her what she was going to do on this very special day, and if she planned on having a party or going out to enjoy herself. She responded that she didn't have any money for a party, so she just was just going to stay home. She said since her dad had passed it was hard for her mom, and she hadn't been able to celebrate her birthday with friends for more than two years. This woman was everything I was looking for, so my response to her was immediate. I told her I wanted to buy her something for her birthday, and I wanted her to go and get it. What I did was Western Union her $100. Now, I had to explain what to do because she had no idea what I was talking about.

I told her to go and get the money and go out and have a party, buy a cake and invite her friends; this was my gift to her. I could tell by her reaction that this meant so much to her, and it also showed her how I cared and wanted her to have a nice birthday. A few days went by while she planned the party, and then the day finally came. When I went online she was there waiting for me as usual and I asked her how it went. She said it was the best time and she had bought a lot of fruit and a cake and all her friends brought her gifts. I had just made this birthday very special for her, and I felt wonderful that I could do it for her. Then I asked her if she had any money left over. She said yes, so I told her now to go out and buy herself something special. This was a gift from me to her. She said she would do it the next day.

What a surprise I had coming to me when we talked again. When I asked her what she bought, the answer came as such a shock. It was a cam; she had gone out and spent the money I gave her so that I could see her when we talked. She said this would make our conversations more enjoyable, and she wanted me to see her when we talked. Now this touched my heart very deeply, and this woman was starting to show me values and love I had never seen before, and it's through this gesture from her that I fell even deeper in love with her.

So if they have a cam or can purchase one, it's a great tool for making a lasting impression and creating a close bond between you and possible mate.

Pictures

Pictures are pictures; they just show whatever is going on at that particular moment in time and freeze it. They're not very personable, nor do they show emotions. They can also be adjusted, modified, and altered to make the image appear better than reality. When you get a picture from a woman, try to get more than one, as more will show the real image of her. You see, while you're looking through the dating site you will see her main picture and you will think to yourself, "This woman is beautiful and perfect." After all, this is the very first thing that will catch your attention. But remember that just as you will select your picture from a group of shots, they have selected theirs the same way. Too many times I have seen a woman's picture and thought she looked perfect, but then when I went into her profile I found she had more shots and by looking through them I saw her differently, and it changed my decision to contact her.

You can't go just by a single picture. You must also read about her in her profile and make sure that if you choose her, somewhere along your conversations you get another photo, hopefully not altered and taken by herself or an amateur photographer. If she can't produce another picture, or comes up with excuses, then I would say there is at least a 90-percent chance she isn't who she claims to be, or she doesn't have the interest in you to get you one. This type of woman uses someone else's snapshot to engage in conversations and just wants someone to like her; she uses this technique so she will be able to talk with men who normally wouldn't have e-mailed her. Or she's part of a scam, trying to lure you into believing she is this person in the picture so she can get money from you for a passport, visa, or some other made-up idea. You need to look at the picture and see if it was professionally done. You will know these as there are no flaws, the women are all posed perfectly, and of course the picture has been adjusted so she looks like an angel. Some women will spend a lot of money for these photos to show their inner beauty, so I'm told, and to help lure a respectable husband.

If you look through her profile and see that she has even more pictures and they look natural, then chances are you will be all right. But still insist on another picture after your first few e-mails, and then some more from time to time, as you want to see her as she looks now, not six months ago. Too many times I have gotten full-body pictures, which are the best of course at displaying the whole person, and the woman looked exactly like what I wanted, but after talking with her for a few months and finally getting a recent photo I found she had gained fifty pounds, which made not a woman I desired. It's very important that you get this from her; don't waste your time talking with a bearded or tattooed man sitting in his bathroom trying to persuade you to send him some money. A later chapter will discuss scams in more detail. Know who you're dealing with before you get too far and before any feelings develop, and you'll do just fine.

Chapter 7

How to Use Instant Messenger Services

Three major messenger services are widely used. Well, OK, a fourth one does exist, but I won't go into any detail about it because I have yet to find a woman who wanted to talk with me on it. But just so you know it's referred to as ICQ. I will list each one of the other services that are commonly used and explain how to download the programs, and walk you through how to use them.

After you read this chapter, I would suggest you download all the programs so that you're ready to go when the women start responding to you and your level of understanding of how they work is greater. You can also try some chat sites just to hone your skills, but I don't suggest looking for a woman on these. I have talked with people on them, and they are usually not the type of person you want to talk with; most of the time, in fact, I found them to be very undesirable. It will, however, allow you to see how the messaging system works, and who cares if you're just starting to learn? They don't know you. It will also allow you to see some of the words they use as a form of shorthand to communicate. Want to know a few? OK, here are some to get you started:

- ttyl: talk to you later
- cu: see you
- lol: laugh out loud
- lmao: laugh my ass off
- u: you
- ru: are you
- brb: be right back

- sri: sorry
- hehe: snicker
- haha: laugh
- muah: kiss

These are just a few, but they're most of the ones you'll encounter throughout your communication. Of course you won't be a pro yet, but at least you can carry your way through a conversation with her.

All right, let's start off with the first messenger service, and then I will talk about the other two briefly.

AIM

This messaging system is provided through America Online, and it will cost you nothing. All you have to do is go to aol.com, see the messaging icon and select it. You will be asked to select a user name; this can be whatever you want except for those that have been already used. Think of something that you would like to be known as, and if it's already being used then add some numbers to it or even a hyphen between words. Make sure you select the right software platform for the download to your computer, by which I mean Macintosh or Windows.

Once it's all loaded you're ready to try it, so run the program. When it starts, a window should pop up for you to add your user name and password. You can even select to save the password so it doesn't ask you for it every time, but that's up to you. If you have other people using your computer I don't recommend this option, as it will allow other people to log on with your name. But make the password something you can easily remember, or at least write it down whether you choose to save it or not. Believe me, it's very hard to remember each password that you use in your everyday life.

OK, you opened the program and logged on; now a long window should appear on the right side of your monitor. You won't have any friends in it yet, but it will have a few groups already there and I would suggest you click on the lower right corner where it says "setup" and delete them. You can do this by placing your pointer on each one and highlighting it, and then clicking on the "delete" button. Let's pretend we have a person to add to our new list. It's very simple to do: Click on "setup" again. Then click on "add a group"; a box should appear where you can add the information for this person. In my system, say her name is Allison and she is twenty-two and lives in Utah. I would name my group Allison 22 Utah, then left-click anywhere in the area inside the window and the group would be added. Then you want to add the sign name of your new friend, so select "add buddy" and type the name exactly as it was given to you. Again click anywhere in the white area inside the box. Now you're all done. You just added this person, and when she comes online and uses the service her name will show up under the buddy's name. When she does come online, all you have to do is go to her name and double-click on it. A message box will open on the screen with your cursor blinking in the text area. Type your message and hit the "enter" key or left-click "send" on the right side of the text box. Seems simple enough, doesn't it?

It's really easy to use, but let's talk for a few minutes about some other features you may want to make this more personal. Click on "My AIM" at the top left corner of the buddy list window; here are some things you may want to use. I'll just discuss the ones I frequently used and wanted to change, and you can look at the others later.

Under "My AIM" you see "away message"; click on this and a drop-down box will appear. Now you have a choice of creating a message explaining why you're not at your computer or tell someone that you're online but busy doing something. Or you can select one that is already preset with basic reasons. Move your pointer over to "away" and click on "new message." You will be asked to label the message, and then inside the lower window add your message there. In the right corner you can select to save this message for later. Once you click "I'm away" the box will stay on the screen unless you minimize it, and a message letter will appear next to your name on your friends' buddy windows. They can right-click on your name and select "get buddy info," and this will tell them what you're doing or why you are away. Or they can send you a message now, and it will appear in the "I'm away" window and tell you they tried to talk with you and left the message. Another option is go back to "My AIM" again and select "edit profile." This has many things you can do; I'm not going to go through each one, but let's talk about a couple. When you select "edit profile" you can allow someone to search for you by clicking the upper left box and then entering your information in. This is seldom if at all used by me, but you can use it if you like; if not, just click "next."

You can also choose to allow other people with AIM to search for you based on your interests, and you can add this feature by selecting the white box in the left top corner and then selecting your interests in each of the drop-down boxes. Once again, if you don't want to do this, just click the "next" button. Now you've come to your personal information box; here you can enter anything you want your new friends to know about you. People can get very imaginative, and there are services that allow you to expand this even further and have many sub-profiles where you can enter all sorts of information.

But none of this is necessary for what we're trying to achieve, and if you want to add this then you will have to search it out for yourself. All I would use is strictly the info box, but even then you don't have to enter anything; it's totally up to you. But on the other hand, if you want to see other people's information you can very easily go to their name once they are online, and right-click on their sign-on name and select "buddy info." Any information they posted will come up. Whether you entered a profile or not, just click on "finish" and this will save it and close the box.

The next thing we will talk about under "My AIM" will be the "edit options," so click this and another box will appear. You can see all the items you can select for your options. The only one you need to know how to use right now is "edit preferences." Select this and yet another box will appear; amazing, isn't it? Most of these options, if you select the tabs, will allow you to turn specific things on or off; these are just some features that you may or may not want, based on your choices. The one I want you to select is "font." This will allow you to pick the type, color, and size of text that appears when you are talking in a window with someone. You can also pick the color you want in the window background, so choose a window color and a text color that go well together so the other person can read your messages easily. Otherwise, just leave it the way it is and it will have a white background and black text by default. I don't suggest you use the text magnification, as it won't help you in talking and is a function I never used, but it's your choice. Try it and see if you like it; you can always go back to the way it was.

The next two tabs I want to talk with you about are "file transfer" and "file sharing." You need these set to "allow"; click on the white circle next to the word to do so. This will let other people you're talking with share files with you. "File transfer" must also be selected to allow pictures and files to go back and forth between your computers, so make sure this is selected by clicking on the white circle by the people on your buddy list, or the one by "allow all users." Now with this done, look at the top of the window. Do you see where it says the directory where the files will go when I receive them? Click on "browse" and go to the folder you want them to be downloaded into. Or click on "make a new folder," create one wherever you want on your drive, then when someone sends you a file or a picture it will be transferred to this folder.

Oh, I almost forgot—there is another important item on the preferences list. You need to make sure that it's enabled, too, and that's the "IM image tab." Select this tab and you can turn on this feature to open a "start dialog" box or a "display status" box, which will show you that the file is transferring and how much is left until it's done. Now there are two other white circles that must be in the "allow" position. One is labeled "when others send me an IM Image" and the other is "for users not on my buddy list." I made sure they were both set on "allow."

That's all you need to know at this point to set AIM up to talk and transfer files. It's not a complete chapter on how to learn everything about the messenger service, but just an overview of how to personalize it a bit and talk with your new friends.

I'll tell you one last thing: If you go to "setup" again for your buddy list, you can right-click on any sign-in name you have, and then select "block buddy." This will stop the program from telling you when this person is online, and the blocked person will no longer know if you're on, either. So if you meet a woman and you don't want to talk with her anymore, don't delete her name, just block her. Otherwise she will know you're online and can still continue to annoy you. But don't worry; if things change, you can always go back to her name and right-click on it again and remove the block.

Now I'll take a moment to go over a few shortcuts you can use when you're talking within a buddy window. If you don't have a friend yet, then make one up; you can always delete it later. Double-click on it and a message window box will appear; you can see when it opens the cursor is automatically placed in the text box. Now just above that are some buttons. The first one changes your text color. The next one, moving right, is to change the color of your window, and you can do this at any time. The next three are to increase your font size, and as you click on each one your text will appear bigger. The next one makes your text italic, and the last one is to change your text so it underlines your words. But remember, all these changes will only be there while you're talking with this person, and if you close the window and then open a new one, it will default back to the preferences you set earlier. The next button will allow you to add a link, such as a Web address. The next one looks like a mountain with a sun. Yes, you guessed it, you can use this to send images or files to your friend. But remember when you select this that they have to approve to receive the files before it will work.

The second-to-last button will take you to a site from which you can send a card or greeting to a friend; you can even send it to her e-mail if you like. And finally, the last button is a smiley face; you will use this one very often. When you click on this, it will open a box and let you select a smiley to show some emotion you may be feeling and add the smiley to your text area; then you simply click "send" or depress the "enter" key to send it.

The last shortcuts are below your text box. There are three buttons. Use the "block" button to block this member from talking with you, as we discussed earlier. The "talk" button will allow you to use a microphone and headset. You can theoretically use this to talk with each other rather then calling from a phone, but this didn't function very well for me and I rarely used it. But you can try it, if you like, as a means of talking to your buddy rather than calling long-distance. The last box that is "get info"; once selected it will show you your buddy's profile information with just a click of a button.

Yahoo

This messaging software functions basically the same way as AIM; to download it you just go to yahoo.com on the Internet. You need to add the same things as with AIM, including the sign-on name and password. I use the same one for all my messenger services to simplify things; the choice is up to you.

Yahoo has a "login" button instead of "My AIM." Here you can set an away message, but one feature Yahoo has that AIM doesn't is "invisible mode." I used this feature all the time; with it, you can see who comes online but they cannot tell that you're on, and yet you can contact anyone you want to. This is a nice feature that's available on both Yahoo and MSN. You will need to use it so you won't have ten or more women trying to talk with you all at once. I talked briefly about the chaos this can cause in previous chapters.

You should now click on "my profiles." This will take you to a profile page on the Internet where you can enter information about yourself, and even post a picture if you like. I liked this feature because when you add a friend, you can right-click on her sign-on name and look at her profile and see information and even a picture if she posted one. Your next move is to click on "tools" and move your pointer to the "manage friends" list, then click on "add a group" just like I explained to you in AIM. Once you've added the information, click on "add a friend." The difference here between AIM and Yahoo is that the person you're adding will be told that you're adding her to your list. She can either accept or reject you, and if she is not online at that time it will add her name to your list. If she comes on later and hits "accept" when the dialog comes up, then she will remain on your list; but if she chooses to reject your request, her name will be removed automatically.

Another feature I liked to use was also under the "tools" button: click on this, then go down to "message archive." If you click on this feature you can save everything that is said between you and the other person during your conversations. I liked this one especially if I was given a phone number and couldn't find it or remember it. But be aware that it only saves conversations for the computer you're talking with them on, and it will overwrite them once it's full. So if you wish to keep the conversations longer, copy and paste them to a word processing file and save them for later.

Another nice feature with Yahoo that the other services don't have is if you double-click on someone who's not online, and type her a message, when she returns she will still get what you said to her. It will show up when anyone sends an offline message, and it will appear when she logs on in a box labeled "offline messages." This was nice for me, because I would say things even when the woman I was looking for wasn't around and she would always get them later. That's about all I will tell you about Yahoo messenger's main window, as the rest is very similar to AIM.

Now let's look at the shortcuts available through the message window. If you double-click on one of your new friends—but remember, you can't make a phony one for a test like you did in AIM—a pop-up window will appear. It's about the same as in AIM except for a few differences. One is that just above the text box is a button labeled "environment"; here you can select a background for your text messages or maybe play a game. There are many to choose from and you should try them all. The one I most frequently used was the "falling hearts" environment; it was very romantic and set the mood for our conversations. But of course the first one you will have is your basic white background, and as time goes on and you win her over, use the falling hearts. It works great for creating an in-love atmosphere. In each environment, if you go to the top toolbar you will see a button called "friend." If you select "buzz friend," watch the screen. A huge kiss will be displayed on the monitor complete with sound! I used this a lot, as it was a very nice way to show affection. There is also a button labeled "webcam." Yes, that's right! Now if you have yours set up on your computer and if she has one, you can click here and either one of you can view the other. Yahoo also allows voice communication with a microphone and a headset, although as stated earlier I didn't find this appealing when talking with the women. The button is labeled "voice."

Let's go now to the lower tool bar. It's basically the same as AIM with the exception of allowing you to change the font of your text. What did I use? I liked Comic sans ms, but you should select whatever you want. The last fun feature I have found with Yahoo is its assortment of smileys; what makes them better than the other messengers' is that they are animated. If you select a kissing smiley, it puckers and kisses the other person. Those are about the only differences between these two messenger services that you need to know right off hand. Let's go on to the last one, shall we?

MSN

MSN is the same type of messenger software as AIM and Yahoo, with the exception of the features being located or labeled differently. And of course it goes without saying that you have to download it at msn.com. So let's briefly talk about a few of the differences to help you use this software.

Under "file" you have to go to "my status" to set an away message. The only difference with MSN is it doesn't allow you to add a customized message. But like Yahoo it does allow you to appear to be offline even when you're not. To add a group you go to "contacts" and "manage groups," then go down to "create group" and enter the information on the woman you're adding. It's the same for her sign-on name, with the exception that you have to enter her entire e-mail address now in full and it must be an MSN account. Just like Yahoo, when you add a person she will be alerted that you added her, but MSN won't give her the option to deny you. You add a person under "add a contact," and once you do this, select her name by clicking on it. Put the new name in the group you just made by left-clicking on it, and while holding down your left mouse button drag your pointer to the new group you added. When the group is highlighted release your finger; this way you've put this person in her group name. MSN also allows you to view a webcam and I found this to be the best software when communicating by video, as the refresh rate is the fastest I've seen so far. And just like the other two, you you can communicate with a headset and a microphone. The smileys in MSN are not as good as Yahoo's and are not animated. So they really don't have the effect on the other person that I feel is necessary.

One thing you can do with MSN unlike the other programs is to click on "tools" at the top of the window, and then when the box opens click "options." At the top you will see "display name"; by default it will have your sign-on name. You can change this any time you want, even adding the smileys and icons that MSN has available. Another more nice feature this program has that the others don't is if the person is offline you can double-click on her name and send her an e-mail without having to go through the normal steps of opening your mailbox and then typing in her address. MSN also allows you to add a picture of yourself or whatever you like to your message window. You also know if the other person has a cam without her telling you; at the top right corner of the text window you will see a small cam icon. Click on this button and it will ask her if she wants to let you see her; she can only accept or reject your request, so no harm done.

Well, that's all there is to each of these messenger p. Each is a little different in how it adds or changes things. But mostly they all function the same way. If they all worked together they could make one very nice messenger program. But that's not the case.

I hope this has helped you get familiar with each service and made your first use much easier, and enabled you to meet the woman of your dreams.

Chapter 8

Scams and What to Look For

This chapter is on just what it says. You should make sure you read this before venturing off on your quest. I want to keep you from making some of the most common mistakes, most of which I have learned from experience. Although I try to cover most of the common scams, they are changing every day and you must be very careful when communicating with your prospective mate.

Let's start off by creating a common scenario: You received an e-mail from a woman and she's very beautiful and looks like every man's dream. She's your dream, anyway, because after all you contacted her first, and in her e-mail she writes wonderful things that get you excited and happy to talk with her.

Soon she e-mails you and tells you to talk with her on one of the messaging services, and she gives you her screen name. So like any eager man you add her and find her online. Somehow she's right there waiting for you and responds immediately, so you start talking. Now, somewhere within let's say ten to thirty minutes she says you're the man of her dreams, or she's in love with you and wants to be with you forever. Be very leery of this. Proceed with extreme caution, as you're probably being set up by a scam artist. It may even be a man using a sexy female identity.

Wait for somewhere along in the conversation for her to ask you to get her out of her country. Understand that if you contacted her from any of the countries that require a visa, she cannot come here. If she says she needs money for a passport or a visa, she is sticking her hand in your pocket, and you will lose your money. I found most of these instances in the Philippines; I think they make their living off of unsuspecting men like us. But I know now that they cannot travel here. Look at it this way: If they could come here anytime they wished, they would already be here and not talking online with you. The fact is the government regulates their immigration, because of the overwhelming number that would just show up and never leave. Besides, if she's so quick to love you then this woman definitely is not the one you're looking for. At any rate, the only way you're going to get to be with her, if at all, is for you to go to her. You might even suggest this to her now, just to see the response she may give you.

But does this mean you should never send money to a prospective partner? The answer is no! But you should initiate this, and if she asks you for it then something is not right. A real woman wanting marriage and commitment will not want your money. However, let's say you're talking with a woman for some time and she seems sincere, and she talks of her feelings and what she thinks of you and you're interested in her. I have in the past, during conversations with several different women from other countries, found that they are very deprived and lack the things we take for granted here. You may want to offer to do something for her, like sending some flowers without her knowing. This is fine as long as you are the initiator.

For instance, one young lady I was talking with, whom I was very sure was interested in me, stated she could not talk with me anymore in the evening because her mother could not afford to feed her. Before we'd started talking, she would go to her aunt's house and eat there and then return home to sleep. So she said she could no longer talk with me at night because she must return to this schedule. After careful consideration I decided that I would offer to send her some money so that she could buy food and not give up our evening chats. I mean, after all, she didn't ask, and it was our talking that caused the problem, so yes, I sent the money, although not much for me, like $200. To her this was enough to give them weeks of food to live on. So you must make sure that this is something you want to do, and something she has not asked for.

In another instance a woman I was interested in was going to a ball; she was graduating from her college and was talking about how she had nothing nice to wear and I noticed how upset she was. Once again I decided to send her something to allow her to buy a dress and shoes; this showed her that I was serious and that I did care about her. But later I found the relationship wasn't going to work out, because she wanted me to wait five years for her to complete her schooling, a time I was not prepared to wait. So I ended this relationship, not her.

Once I've established contact with a woman, I always send out a second generic e-mail that tells about me, my likes, and what I do for a living, as well as some of the things that I may have not mentioned in my profile. You may remember the example from Chapter 2. I would recommend that you also save yours in a word processing form just as you did your profile and introduction letter. I received more than eighty responses from the all women I contacted, and this is a nice break-the-ice kind of e-mail, so to speak. But also in this message I always send a few more pictures of myself, and ask that they do so, too, when they respond.

You see, you need to make sure they are who they say they are. I ran into a few who, no matter how long I talked with them, had many excuses for not sending a recent pic. How would you like to talk with someone for a few months and never see who it is you're talking to? I went even further with two young ladies from the Philippines. They played the thirty-second I-love-you-and-want-to-be-with-you-forever game, too soon in our conversation. But they couldn't produce pictures, so I told each of them to send me a picture while she was in a bikini, touching her nose and standing on one foot. Sounds crazy, doesn't it? But if they're serious then they would do it. And if they were who they said they were, you wouldn't get to this point. Another thing I push for if they're serious about talking with me is a camera for their computer. I talked about this earlier, but it really helps to stop scams from occurring. You can see whom you're talking to and ensure you're not being taken for a ride. Cams aren't that expensive, either, and if the women are serious about you they will get one. This way you can talk and see each other, and if you're that far along in your relationship, if they can't afford one then send them one. It will be a nice gesture on your part, but also will show them ever more how serious you are.

Nothing beats conversing through an instant messenger service, then looking at them and their reactions at the same time. Of course what I did was call them on the phone and talk to them while at the same time viewing them. This is very nice and makes the conversation more personable. But back to the scams!

Don't think some of the marriage agencies companies aren't looking to scam you to make a quick buck. If you wish to use an agency to meet the woman, then you don't need to be reading this book, but be prepared to buy out the contract she has with them when she finds a mate. You can search out Russian bride scams or dating scams on the Internet and find current information on sites and businesses to watch out for. Also, these sites sometimes have profiles and pictures of women known to take your hard-earned money.

Here's another scam that can occur. You're talking with a young woman and she seems to like you very much, and you have been talking for some time. Along the way something happens to her or her family and they're in desperate need of money for surgery or to recover from some type of catastrophic event. She asks for help, talks about selling her home or furnishings or whatever the case may be to get you to feel sorry for her. Who knows what she will do to try to persuade you to help her or her family? Well, this is a difficult choice to make; if for some reason you decide to help, then try to find some way to validate what she is saying. Like where is the hospital? What is its name? Who can you contact to make things right? Try everything you can to get some means of calling the institution or person involved. Even I have fallen into this trap. I learned the hard way, and let me tell you it wasn't a cheap lesson. So unless you can verify the situation or you have the ability to go there to see her and help her while you're there, then just give it up.

I wouldn't send anything if I were you! Especially if you never have met this woman before, or you cannot validate her story. Believe me, they can be very creative, but if she's telling the truth then something can be done to verify it. But the risk is still there and it's your choice.

Now let's talk about translator fees and such. At some point you're going to be told about translation fees that are associated with your correspondence. Now, some of these are valid and the girls do have to pay to have your messages translated from English to whatever and then back for you. But you must be very careful of this; there are agencies out there that pose as individual women and ask you to pay for this service. It's normally $5-$10 dollars for an e-mail sent back and forth, but it depends on whether photos are involved or not.

How can you tell if they're legitimate or not? Well, good luck. The only means that I can see is this: You can translate the letters with software that's available online for free; some of them run from the Web site and you don't need to download. But they have a hard time interpreting some languages, mainly Chinese and Russian, from what I can see. Just type in "translator" under the search bar and you'll find a few. Some legitimate agencies obviously will get upset if you try to take their money away from them, so unless the women can access a computer somewhere like in a coffee shop or library, or they have one at home, this can prove to be useless.

What you can do if you're far enough into the relationship is start calling her on the phone. Yes, it may difficult to speak with her, but some women are very fluent. You'll have to see what your woman's language level is. If I decided to do such a thing without ever meeting the woman, I would send her flowers without telling her about it and see if she got them. If they arrive and she tells you that she received them, then you've verified she has told the truth on that.

The key here is verification of who they are before sending any money. If you have successfully verified that she is who she says she is, then I would check out the different interpretation fees and decide what would be the best way for you to go. Some will let you pay monthly, which is nice, and if you send e-mails back and forth each day as well as photos, this can save you money. But the one I liked was the one where they used the money per you correspondence. This for me was better as she responded only once a week, so costwise this was the better deal for me. But each agency's policies and costs are different, so you will have to contact the one you're dealing with for that information.

When it comes to scams, no matter what you watch for or try to inhibit, unscrupulous people may still try to take advantage of you. But at least you have some idea of what to watch out for. The best method all in all is to find a woman in a country that doesn't require a visa; after all, if she wants to come here and cannot pay, you can pay her way with a major credit card. This protects you, as she must go to the airport and get the ticket and she cannot sell it or transfer it if the usual restrictions are imposed. If the ticket is never used you can sometimes get a refund, or a credit toward another flight. But once again, every airline is different and refund or cancellation policies are variable; you should check with each one before you decide to purchase tickets. Ask their policy before booking the flight so you know what will happen if the passenger doesn't take the flight.

Even the most careful person may have some bad experiences, but there should be even fewer now that you have read this information. As with dating a woman from your own state, there is some cost of developing and maintaining the relationship; sometimes you spend the money and take her out and end up with nothing. So you should think of working through the Internet in the same way; it's just that this woman is a little further away and courtship requires more work.

Then again, you're looking for something more, and of course a more refined and attractive woman. Even I have spent a few thousands dollars in my search; I have had some wonderful experiences, but still often came up empty-handed. But remember that the best part of this type of relationship is when you actually get to go wherever she lives, or you bring her to you. That's definitely where the investment pays off.

Chapter 9

Visas, Passports, and Other Details

From what I can gather, visas are three things. One, they are permission for you to enter another country. Two, they are a way for the country to make some extra money on your visit. And three, they help keep track of who enters and when they leave. As I stated before, it is very difficult for any woman who is young and attractive to get a visa to the U.S. And as I have also told you in the previous chapters, this is because of the huge number of women who would come over here and never leave; they want to escape their country and come to the land of the free. Could you imagine how this would disrupt our already out-of-balance status with marriages and the family unit? I mean, if hundreds and thousands of young, beautiful women entered here every day searching for a husband, what a mess this would be for the economy, not to mention the current marriages that are in danger now of failing.

But did I say they cannot get a visa? If they are young and travel with their family, say, for vacation, it may be allowed. Or if they have some ties to their country, such as property or owning a business that would require them to go back, then they may obtain a visa. Or let's say if they were to apply for an F1 visa or the green card lottery they may be able to get in, but the requirements and length of time involved don't make such a visa desirable.

OK, so let's talk briefly about what visas are available and see what can possibly work for you. As you check into this, I think you will find the K1 fiancée or K3 visa is what you will end up with, unless she is in America already on a visa of her own. This definitely would make it very easy to be with her, but it's a rarity. These women are actually here in the United States, but you have to look hard to find them.

Here is a list of the most commonly requested types of visas:

- B: temporary visitor for business or pleasure
- F: student (academic or language program)
- M: student in vocational or recognized non-academic program
- H: individuals in specialty occupations (e.g., nurses)
- L: intra-company transfer
- J: exchange visitor
- K: fiancé(e) of U.S. citizen
- O: individuals with extraordinary ability in sciences, arts, education, business, athletics
- Q: participant in an international cultural program
- D: crew (airline/ship)
- R: religious workers
- I: journalists
- C: transit through U.S.

As you can see, many types can be applied for, but I will discuss only those relevant to bringing the woman of your dreams to you. If there is another you would like to know more, visit the American consulate's Web page.

The following is INS information pulled from the Internet. This is for generic reference only; you should check official government Web sites for updates and changes.

F1 visas

No alien may be issued an F-1 visa to attend a U.S. public elementary or middle school (K-8). Any alien who wishes to attend public high school (grades 9–12) in the United States in student visa (F-1) status must submit evidence that the local school district has been reimbursed in advance for the unsubsidized per capita cost of the education. Also, attendance at U.S. public high schools cannot exceed a total of twelve months. No alien may be issued an F-1 visa in order to attend a publicly funded adult education program.

The student visa applicant must have successfully completed a course of study normally required for enrollment. The student, unless coming to participate exclusively in an English language training program, must either be sufficiently proficient in English to pursue the intended course of study, or the school must have made special arrangements for English language courses or teach the course in the student's native language.

Applicants must also prove that sufficient funds are or will be available from an identified and reliable financial source to defray all living and school expenses during the entire period of anticipated study in the United States. Specifically, applicants must prove they have enough readily available funds to meet all expenses for the first year of study, and that adequate funds will be available for each subsequent year of study. M-1 student visa applicants must have evidence that sufficient funds are immediately available to pay all tuition and living costs for the entire period of intended stay.

An applicant coming to the United States to study must be accepted for a full course of study by an educational institution approved by the Bureau of Citizenship and Immigration Services in the Department of Homeland Security (BCIS). The institution must send to the applicant a Form I-20A-B, Certificate of Eligibility for Nonimmigrant (F-1) Student Status for Academic and Language Students. The nonacademic or vocational institution must send to the student a Form I-20M-N, Certificate of Eligibility for Nonimmigrant (M-1) Student Status For Vocational Students. Educational institutions obtain Forms I-20A-B and I-20M-N from the BCIS.

The nonimmigrant visa application Form DS-156 lists classes of people who are ineligible under U.S. law to receive visas. In some instances an applicant who is ineligible, but who is otherwise properly classifiable as a student, may apply for a waiver of ineligibility and be issued a visa if the waiver is approved.

To applying for a student visa, go to the INS Web site and select Applying—Student Visas and review the section "When Do I Need to Apply for My Student Visa" to find important information about timeframes for applying for a student visa. Applicants for student visas should generally apply at the U.S. embassy or consulate with jurisdiction over their place of permanent residence. Although visa applicants may apply at any U.S. consular office abroad, it may be more difficult to qualify for the visa outside the country of permanent residence.

Each applicant for a student visa must pay a nonrefundable $100 application fee and submit:

- An application Form DS-156, together with a Form DS-158. Both forms must be completed and signed. Some applicants will also be required to complete and sign Form DS-157. A separate form is needed for children, even if they are included in a parent's passport. The DS-156 must be the February 2003 date, either the electronic "e-form application" or the non-electronic version. At the Web site, select "Nonimmigrant Visa Application Form DS-156" to access both versions of the DS-156. Applicants may also check with the embassy consular section where they will apply to determine if the hard copy blank DS-156 form is available should they need it.
- A passport valid for travel to the United States and with a validity date at least six months beyond the applicant's intended period of stay in the United States. If more than one person is included in the passport, each person desiring a visa must make an application.
- One 2x2 photograph. At the Web site, see the photo format explained in "nonimmigrant photograph requirements."
- For the "F" applicant, a Form I-20A-B. For the "M" applicant, a Form I-20M-N.
- Evidence of sufficient funds.

Student visa applicants must also establish to the satisfaction of the consular officer that they have binding ties to a residence in a foreign country that they have no intention of abandoning, and that they will depart the United States when they have completed their studies. It is impossible to specify the exact form the evidence should take since applicants' circumstances vary greatly.

Applicants should be aware that a visa does not guarantee entry into the United States. The Directorate of Border and Transportation Security has authority to deny admission. Also, the Directorate of Border and Transportation Security, not the consular officer, determines the period for which the bearer of an exchange visitor visa is authorized to remain in the United States. At the port of entry, a Directorate of Border and Transportation Security official validates Form I-94, Record of Arrival-Departure, which notes the length of stay permitted

An F-1 student may not accept off-campus employment at any time during the first year of study; however, the BCIS may grant permission to accept off-campus employment after one year. F-1 students may accept on-campus employment from the school without BCIS permission. Except for temporary employment for practical training, an M-1 student may not accept employment.

A spouse and unmarried minor children may also be classified for a nonimmigrant visa to accompany or follow the student. Family members must meet all visa eligibility requirements, including evidence that they will have sufficient funds for their support, and that they will depart the U.S. when the student's program ends. Spouses and children of students may not accept employment at any time.

Questions on how to obtain Forms I-20A-B and I-20M-N should be made to the educational institution. If the institution does not have the forms, it needs to contact the local BCIS office

Fiancée visa

A citizen of a foreign country who would like to come to the United States to marry an American citizen and reside in the U.S. will have to obtain a K-1 visa. To establish K-1 visa classification for an alien fiancée, an American citizen must file a petition, Form I-129F, Petition for Alien Fiancé, with the Bureau of Citizenship and Immigration Services in the Department of Homeland Security (BCIS) having jurisdiction over the place of the petitioner's residence in the United States. Such petitions may not be adjudicated abroad. The approved petition will be forwarded by BCIS to the American consular office where the alien fiancée will apply for her visa. A petition is valid for a period of four months from the date of BCIS action, and may be revalidated by the consular officer.

Applicants who have a communicable disease, or have a dangerous physical or mental disorder; are drug addicts; have committed serious criminal acts including crimes involving moral turpitude, drug trafficking, and prostitution; are likely to become a public charge; have used fraud or other illegal means to enter the United States; or are ineligible for citizenship, must be refused a visa. The two-year foreign residency requirement for former exchange visitors is also applicable. If the applicant is found to be ineligible, the consular officer will advise her if the law provides for a waiver.

The consular officer will notify the beneficiary when the approved petition is received and provide to the beneficiary the necessary forms and instructions to apply for a "K" visa. A fiancée visa applicant is an intending immigrant and, therefore, must meet documentary requirements similar to the requirements of an immigrant visa applicant. The following documents are normally required:

- valid passport
- birth certificate
- divorce or death certificate of any previous spouse
- police certificate from all places lived since age sixteen
- medical examination
- evidence of support
- evidence of valid relationship with the petitioner
- two photographs 1.5 inches square (37x37mm), showing full face, against a light background

Both petitioner and beneficiary must be legally able and willing to conclude a valid marriage in the United States. The petitioner and beneficiary must have previously met in person within the past two years unless the Attorney General waives that requirement. As soon as the processing of a case is completed and the applicant has all necessary documents, a consular officer will interview the fiancée. If she is found eligible, a visa will be issued, valid for one entry during a period of six months. A non-refundable $100 application fee is collected.

After entry into the U.S., the alien fiancée must apply for work authorization with the BCIS. The marriage must take place within ninety days of admission into the United States. Following the marriage, the alien spouse must apply to the BCIS to establish a record of entry for conditional permanent residence status. After two years, the alien may apply to the BCIS for removal of the conditional status.

The unmarried minor children of a K-1 beneficiary derive "K-2" nonimmigrant visa status from the parent so long as the children are named in the petition. A separate petition is not required if the children accompany or follow the alien fiancée within one year from the date of issuance of the K-1 visa. Thereafter, a separate immigrant visa petition is required. For employment, the alien fiancée must apply for work authorization with the BCIS.

For questions on where to obtain the Form I-129F petition, and how and where to file it, contact your local BCIS office for details. For questions on processing the visa application at the American consular office overseas, contact that consular office.

B1/B2 (business) visa

The B1 or B2 visitor visa is a nonimmigrant visa for foreign citizens desiring to enter the United States temporarily for business (B1, business travel visa) or for pleasure or medical treatment (B2, tourist visa). People planning to travel to the U.S. for a different purpose, such as students, temporary workers, crewmen, journalists, etc., must apply for a different visa in the appropriate category. Travelers from certain eligible countries may also be able to visit the U.S. without a visa on the Visa Waiver Program (see Chapter 1 for a list of visa waiver countries).

Applicants for B1 business or B2 tourist visas have the burden of showing that they qualify for such visa. The presumption is that every visitor visa applicant is an intending immigrant. Therefore, applicants for B1 or B2 visas must convince the consular officer the temporary nature of their trip by demonstrating that:

- the purpose of their trip is to enter the U.S. for business, pleasure, or medical treatment;
- they plan to remain for a specific, temporary period of time;
- they have a residence outside the U.S., as well as other strong economic, financial, and family ties to their home country that will insure their return abroad at the end of the visit.

Applicants for B1 business or B2 tourist visas should generally apply at the American embassy or consulate with jurisdiction over their place of permanent residence. Although visa applicants may apply at any U.S. consular office abroad, it may be more difficult to qualify for the visa outside the country of residence.

Applicants for the B1 or B2 visa must pay a nonrefundable $100 application fee, plus any reciprocity fee applicable to the applicant's country, and submit:

- Form DS156, Nonimmigrant Visa Application, completed and signed.
- A passport valid for travel to the United States and with a validity date at least six months beyond the applicant's intended period of stay in the United States. If more than one person is included in the passport, each person desiring a visa must complete an application.
- One photograph, two inches square (50x50 mm) for each applicant, showing full face, without head covering, against a light background.
- For all male nonimmigrant visa applicants between the ages of sixteen and forty-five, regardless of nationality and regardless of where they apply, a Form DS157, Supplement Visa Application, in addition to the DS156. Some American embassies and consulates also require female and other male applicants to complete the Form DS157. Applicants from state sponsors of terrorism age sixteen and over, irrespective of gender, without exception are required to complete the DS157. Seven countries are now designated as state sponsors of terrorism, including North Korea, Cuba, Syria, Sudan, Iran, Iraq, and Libya.

Note that each American Embassy and Consulate has different visa application procedures and requirements. You should contact the consulate or an immigration attorney for information regarding the local rules.

Applicants must also present evidence that shows the purpose of the trip, intent to depart the United States, and arrangements made to cover the costs of the trip. It is impossible to specify the exact form the evidence should take since applicants' circumstances vary greatly.

People traveling to the U.S. on business can present a letter from the U.S. company indicating the purpose of the trip, the applicant's intended length of stay, and the company's intent to pay travel expenses. People traveling to the U.S. as tourists may use letters from relatives or friends in the U.S. whom the applicant plans to visit, or present documents showing participation in a planned tour. People traveling to the U.S. for medical treatment should have a statement from a doctor or institution concerning proposed medical treatment.

Those applicants who do not have sufficient funds to support themselves while in the U.S. must present convincing evidence that an interested person will provide financial support. Visitors are not permitted to accept employment during their stay in the U.S. Depending on individual circumstances, applicants may provide other evidence substantiating the trip's purpose and specifying the nature of binding obligations, such as family ties or employment, that would compel their return to their country.

A person whose passport contains a previously issued visitor visa may qualify for special expedited procedures available at most U.S. embassies or consulates for issuance of a new B1 or B2 visa. Unless previously canceled, a visa is valid until its expiration date. Therefore, if the traveler has a valid U.S. B1 or B2 visa in an expired passport, he or she may use it along with a new valid passport for travel and admission to the United States.

Attempting to obtain a visa by the willful misrepresentation of a material fact, or fraud, may result in the permanent refusal of a visa or denial of entry into the United States.

If the consular officer should find it necessary to deny the issuance of a visitor visa, the applicant may apply again if there is new evidence to overcome the basis for the refusal. In the absence of new evidence, consular officers are not obliged to reconsider such cases.

Applicants should be aware that a visa does not guarantee entry into the United States. At the port of entry, an immigration inspector must authorize the traveler's admission to the U.S. The inspector has authority to deny admission. Also, the inspector will determine how long the person is permitted to stay in the United States. If she is admitted, the inspector will issue the traveler a Form I-94, Record of Arrival/Departure, which notes the length of stay permitted. Those visitors who wish to stay beyond the time indicated on their Form I-94 must apply for an extension of stay with the U.S. Citizenship and Immigration Services (USCIS) in the United

States. The decision to grant or deny a request for extension of stay is made solely by the USCIS.

Passports

Passports are your identity papers and you cannot leave the country without them; they are required for you to re-enter the United States, as well as to enter any other country you are visiting. You must apply for your passport well before your trip. Here is some general information on how and where to apply.

You must provide Form DS-11, Application for Passport, and present proof of U.S. citizenship with any one of the following:

- previous U.S. passport (mutilated, altered, or damaged passports are not acceptable as evidence of U.S. citizenship)
- certified birth certificate issued by the city, county, or state (note: a certified birth certificate has a registrar's raised, embossed, impressed, or multicolored seal, registrar's signature, and the date the certificate was filed with the registrar's office, which must be within one year of your birth)
- Consular Report of Birth Abroad or Certification of Birth
- naturalization certificate
- certificate of citizenship

A Delayed Birth Certificate filed more than one year after your birth may be acceptable if it listed the documentation used to create it and is signed by the attending physician or midwife, or lists an affidavit signed by the parents, or shows early public records.

If you do not have a previous U.S. passport or a certified birth certificate, you will need a Letter of No Record issued by the state with your name, date of birth, years searched for a birth record, and statement that there is no birth certificate on file for you, and as many of the following as possible:

- baptismal certificate
- hospital birth certificate
- census record
- early school record
- family bible record
- doctor's record of post-natal care

These documents must be early public records showing the date and place of birth, preferably created within the first five years of your life.

You may also submit an Affidavit of Birth, form DS-10, from an older blood relative, that is, a parent, aunt, uncle, or sibling, who has personal knowledge of your birth. It must be notarized or have the seal and signature of the acceptance agent.

If you were born abroad and do not have a Consular Report of Birth Abroad or Certificate of Birth on file, then:

- If you claim citizenship through birth abroad to one U.S. citizen parent, you will need a foreign birth certificate, proof of citizenship of your U.S. citizen parent, and an affidavit of your U.S. citizen parent showing all periods and places of residence or physical presence in the United States and abroad before your birth.
- If you claim citizenship through birth abroad to two U.S. citizen parents, you will need your foreign birth certificate, parents' marriage certificate, and proof of citizenship of your U.S. parents and an affidavit of your U.S. citizen parents showing all periods and places of residence of physical presence in the United States and abroad before your birth.

Voter registration cards and Army discharge papers are not proof of citizenship.

If you travel extensively, you may request a larger, forty-eight-page passport at no additional cost. To do so, attach a signed request for a forty-eight-page passport to your application.

The citizenship evidence submitted for minors under the age of fourteen must list both parents' names.

In addition to proof of citizenship, you must also prove your identity with any one of these, if you are recognizable:

- previous U.S. passport (mutilated, altered, or damaged passports are not acceptable as proof of identity)
- naturalization certificate
- certificate of citizenship
- current, valid driver's license
- government ID (city, state, or federal)
- military ID (military and dependents)

Note that a Social Security Card does not prove your identity.

If none of these are available, you will need some signature documents, not acceptable alone as ID (for example, a combination of documents, such as your Social Security card, credit card, bank card, library card, etc.), and a person who can vouch for you. He or she must have known you for at least two years, be a U.S. citizen or permanent resident, have valid ID, and fill out a Form DS-71 in the presence of a passport agent.

Each minor child under age fourteen must appear in person. Both parents or legal guardians must present evidence of identity when they apply for a minor under the age of fourteen.

For minors fourteen to seventeen, your child must appear in person. For security reasons, parental consent may be requested. If your child does not have identification of his or her own, you need to accompany your child, present identification, and co-sign the application

Next, you must provide two passport photos. Your photographs must be 2x2 inches in size, identical, taken within the past six months, showing your current appearance, either color or black and white, a full-face front view with a plain white or off-white background, between one inch and 1-3/8 inches from the bottom of the chin to the top of the head, taken in normal street attire (uniforms should not be worn in photographs except religious attire that is worn daily; do not wear a hat or headgear that obscures the hair or hairline). If you normally wear prescription glasses, a hearing device, wig, or similar articles, they should be worn for your picture. Dark glasses or nonprescription glasses with tinted lenses are not acceptable unless you need them for medical reasons. A medical certificate may be required.

Finally, you pay the applicable fee. When applying at one of the thousands of designated application acceptance facilities in the U.S., you pay the application processing fee to the "U.S. Department of State" and the execution fee to the facility where you are applying. When applying at a regional passport agency, both fees are combined into one payment to the "U.S. Department of State."

At this time you must also provide a Social Security Number. If you do not provide your Social Security Number, the Internal Revenue Service may impose a $500 penalty. If you have any questions, call your nearest IRS office.

Other passport and travel tips

Check with your local post offices; they have passport-ordering centers. Make sure you find one with photo capabilities so you don't need to go elsewhere for a photo. If you don't have a birth certificate, then you will need to apply for one. This is the easiest way: if you search on the Internet for "birth certificates" there are literally hundreds of places that will get yours for you and send it through the mail. What I did was go to the Web site of the state I was born in, fill out the information and request a copy. Of course, there was a fee for this and it may change, but I paid a little more than $20, plus delivery. I needed to get it quickly so there was another twenty bucks to overnight it, and I had to be home to sign for it; they will not leave it without a signature.

Once you have your valid birth certificate and a state I.D. or a driver's license, go down to the post office and wait in line. I would suggest going early in the morning on a weekday, as the line may not be so long. Tell the postal employee that you want a passport, and he or she will give you the form to fill out. Don't sign the form until the postal employee tells you to do so! All right, all the information's filled in, so back to the window you go. They'll take your photos and your birth certificate and ID and verify everything again. They will ask you if you want this in the normal processing time of four to six weeks or in only two weeks. The passport with normal processing will cost roughly one hundred bucks. If you go with the two-week option there will be at least $70 added on; ask them the cost and determine which you want.

You won't get your birth certificate back until they have approved your passport and mailed it to you. You will get a receipt, though, and information on how to check on the status of the application, so after two to three weeks you can call and see where it's at in the system. And that's it! The passport process is done and you're well on your way to getting to be with the woman of your dreams, provided you don't still have to apply for the visa.

If you find you need to get a visa, don't sweat it. If you type in a search for the visa through the Internet, you will find hundreds of legitimate sites where you can get a visa as fast as you like. For instance, I searched for the term "China visa." When the results came up there were many to choose from, varying by price, timing, and reputation. I chose one and called them up to verify their authenticity. Then I went back to the Web site and downloaded the application for them to process, as well as the application for the Chinese consulate.

I filled out the form very carefully filled it out, then I collected the items they requested, including the visa picture the same size as a passport photo and a valid passport good for at least six months longer then my stay. All that was left was to decide how I wanted it delivered it back to me, as well as the term and number of entries I wanted the visa to be good for. The service will provide you with a fee sheet; there is a standard fee for each item you pick. I choose to play it safe and picked a double-entry visa. I did this because I would be flying into one city in China, then catching a flight to my destination city in the same country, thinking this could be seen technically as a double entry. But later I found out for China this wasn't necessary unless I were also going to Hong Kong. You should check if this applies to you just to be sure; a country like Russia, for instance, requires a double-entry visa if your plane just lands in one city before you fly to another city in Russia. It is sometimes better to pay a few dollars more and protect yourself from this misfortune.

So I collected all the paperwork and went down to the post office again. Here I reviewed the shipping method with the clerk, and found that registered mail was the best and most secure way to go. So I filled out the address label and paid the $8 fee, and away it went. I also selected rush delivery and two-day shipment back to me, which must be signed for. Don't despair if you're unavailable; you can pick it up at the local post office at your convenience. Doesn't sound too bad, now, does it? Of course, there are other things to consider like lodging, car rentals, and whatnot. But as long as you have on the visa the approximate time you will be going, you will be fine. I chose a six-month entry period just in case my plans changed.

Air fares and travel guides

I won't take a long time going through all of these, but you should search many different airlines or groups online that deal in travel. They can usually find great rates for your destinations, I went through as many of the reputable ones as I could to make my plans. Flights to the U.S. are on special sometimes and you can get some really great deals. Also, if you've picked a woman in the hot spots of travel, you can find very reasonable and cheap flights to these countries.

If you're looking for travel guides you can search online the same way, but usually the service where you buy your flights will have them. Then again, you're meeting and spending time with a woman who can show you around her country knowledgeably. I felt I didn't need to bother with travel books, as my guide was a warm and very charming woman who knew her country well and was happy to show it to me.

Translations and services

You may also want to pick up a translation handbook. This will have common words and phrases for you to use during your stay. Or maybe you can find a business that you can hire that will translate back and forth between you and her for a fee. Believe it or not, these are available and can be found by searching for them in her country, but I think if you're at the point you are right now, you must not need this service because you've been able to communicate pretty well thus far. And if you want to, let's say, talk with her parents, I'm sure she will do that for you at no charge. It would also be a little awkward having a stranger there when you're meeting with the family. Translation can be done for phone conversations, too, although it is costly to have a third party talk between you and your desired mate.

Chapter 10

My Visit to China
(The Start of My Ultimate Experience)

Let's talk about my visit to see a young woman in China. When I first started this adventure I was waiting for my visa to come in. Well, it finally arrived and now all the paperwork I needed was in order, so it came time to schedule the date and time for the flight. I decided to choose a date within three weeks of receiving my passport and visa. I started to book my tickets and schedule the days I would go; I checked various sites on the Internet and all the well-known reduced airline ticket Web pages. What I found out is that everyone I checked was very different in price, and some of them couldn't even help me in my search. I even tried my trusty AAA membership and turned up the same cost figures; the fares were from $3,400 to $7,500. You can see that even for someone that has money to throw away, these prices are unspeakable, so I continued to search more and more but continued to come up empty.

I wanted to try something different and had an idea. During the summer months they were offering really low fares across the United States, so I developed an alternative plan. I found the name of the airline that flew to China, China Southern Airlines. Nearly all the flights from the U.S. to China are sent to Los Angeles first and then to China. So I called China Southern and asked them how much the fare was from Los Angeles to China; they responded with a price of $1,300. Well, they didn't have to say any more. I immediately booked the ticket. Then I called and searched online for a round-trip ticket from Detroit to Los Angeles; I found the best fare through the American Automobile Association, $277.

So you can see that by booking two round-trip fares, one from Detroit to Los Angeles and another from Los Angeles to China, I only spent $1,577. Wow, what a difference from the quoted price of $3,400 to $7,500. So here's a quick tip for you: Check everywhere and by any means you have available, and try to think of each and every possibility for your flight. No matter how close to the date of travel, you can find a better fare just by being a little bit more imaginative.

The Flight

So I was all set, and everything was all ready to start my little adventure. I got up and headed for the airport. My flight to California left at 9 a.m. and got to California at 11 a.m.; not bad — only four hours of flight time, and with the time zone changes I lost only two hours. This arrival made me thirteen hours early for the China flight as they only go out at midnight, but this enabled me to spend some time walking around Los Angeles, plus I saved more than $1,600, so I didn't mind it at all. The flight to China started off with a Boeing 777. This is a huge airplane; I think they refer to it as an airbus, because it easily seats ten people across in most sections and can hold 550 people at maximum capacity. What I found was a completely booked airplane, but the majority of people on it were couples typically in their early thirties to late forties. Later I would discover that they were all going to China because they adopted children there. So the flight over wasn't too bad, and besides, while waiting for my flight I met a very attractive and wonderful woman who was waiting for the baggage check to open and, lucky me, she was on the same flight. Yeah, yeah, I know I was going to see a young woman in China, but I wanted someone to talk with and the timing was excellent.

We hit it off very well from the start and ended up spending the whole time before takeoff talking, and later we checked in together and even made them change our seats so we could sit beside each other on the flight; this made the trip even more enjoyable. She lived in the city I was heading to in China called Guangzhou, so she told me some things about her city and about China that I wasn't aware of.

The flights lasted twelve to thirteen hours. The seats were a bit cramped, but you could get up and walk around after takeoff. Also, of course, they fed you small dinners and gave you plenty of refreshments. They also had a duty-free cart; if you're a smoker like me you could get a carton of cigarettes for only $10. Of course, it was only available when the plane was over China. But the only brands I saw were Marlboro Red and Marlboro White, so a menthol smoker like me had better bring enough for the stay. The flight also included a movie and a few different audio channels, and since the flight left Los Angeles at midnight there was also the option of sleeping through the whole trip.

And here's another useful bit of information for you. From California to China there's a nine-hour difference, so with that and the flight time, after leaving on Friday I got to China on Sunday morning about 9 a.m., which made me lose one whole day. But the good news is that the flight back left around 9 p.m. Friday night and got to California around 7 p.m. Friday, so it would appear that I gained two hours. And let's not forget the flight there with all the people going over to adopt babies; guess what the plane back was full of. Yep, newly adopted, crying and screaming babies. What are the odds of them all not being seated near you, and also not crying their heads off? Good thing the plane has a free goodie bag with ear plugs and shades to cover your eyes. If you want the best trip yet, then I suggest you use them both and sleep. Nighty-night.

My final destination was Nanning, but the first stop I had was Guangzhou. Once I exited the plane I had to walk over and get onto a bus and this gets a bit cramped, They're in the process of building a new airport there, so maybe it will be complete if you venture to this area. The bus took us to the immigration office where I had to submit a quarantine card, which I'd filled out on the plane. It just asked the basic information, making sure that you're not sick. Once I turned this in, I headed over and presented my passport for entry. The line moved very fast and I wasn't asked any questions; they just checked that my paperwork was in order, and I was off to get my bags.

The fun starts if you're traveling somewhere other then Guangzhou, which I was, lucky me. When I exited the airport I had to get a connecting flight. I had no idea what to do to get there, or that there would be ne'er-do-wells waiting for my arrival. There was in fact a Chinese man who approached me and asked if I was connecting to another flight. Unaware of his intent as he was dressed in a suit and nicely groomed, I said yes and showed him my ticket. "Follow me," he said, then he took my luggage and walked away. My flight from LA was late leaving by one hour, so I was close to missing the flight to Nanning. And it's a good thing this fellow came along to help me, or else I would have surely missed my flight. What I didn't know is that in every airport you land in and then fly out of in China there is an airport tax. This guy said it was four hundred yen, which is about $50, and they had a window where you bought the coupon to pay the tax. What I found out later is it was only ninety yen, so the guy screwed me out of $38.75, but even when I finally found out about it weeks later it didn't bother me because if he hadn't helped me I surely would have missed the flight entirely.

But from this point it was fairly simple; I just went to the ticket line for China Southern and the ticket agents had the flight number and destination displayed above each counter. They gave me my boarding pass and checked my luggage, and then I went and paid your airport tax and got a coupon in return. Then I just went through the usual screening as in any airport and headed to the gate. There, they checked that I paid my tax and also verified my flight and ticket. Then, something different I noticed when I boarded the plan was that China Southern had very nicely dressed stewardesses, and they served a meal regardless of the flight time. For me, the extra flight to Nanning was only an hour but they still fed me; this is something the U.S. airlines have eliminated from their flights.

When I arrived in Nanning, I went straight to claim my bag. At the baggage area, I could see that a crowd of people was held back from the luggage area by a small fence. This was set up so they could meet their arriving friends and relatives, and that's when I saw her. There she was, four feet eleven inches and so tiny, maybe seventy-six pounds, jumping up and down and holding roses with the biggest smile she ever had in her life when she saw it was me. I had never had such a wonderful greeting; I thought she was going to bounce through the roof. I was really impatient to get my bag and go over there, as she made me feel like the most wanted and loved man in the world.

As I approached her the excitement grew more and more, so I ran up and hugged her and accepted the flowers. I greeted her aunt and uncle, and we were off to an awaiting taxi. The whole time we were in the taxi she stared at me and had the biggest and warmest smile on her face.

As the taxi drove off I could see the countryside was very green and well taken care of, with no residences to speak of that I could see. Only a few businesses were scattered here and there on the roadside, and not until we came closer to the city did I really see any signs of people. But what I found out as we entered the city was people everywhere. I mean there were thousands of motorcycles, mopeds, bikes, taxicabs, and buses. They were everywhere, and I also noticed that there were no traffic lights. During my stay there I believe I saw only two working lights at any of the intersections. Not even any stop signs. Amazingly enough it seemed to work for the Chinese, but it's really crazy to drive there, and I don't recommend that anyone rent a car in China. Although I had planned to, I was very thankful that one was not available in Nanning. Mostly because with the training we have here in the United States, I would have been stuck at the first intersection for hours. The Chinese drivers all go and don't wait for anything, and with Americans being trained to stop and let the opposing traffic go first, I would never have moved. Trust me, you won't believe it until you see it. Take a taxi and save your sanity. Besides, when you get in a cab it only starts off at seven yen; at today's rates that's about eighty cents, and you can usually get anywhere you need to for less then $2.

The cab pulled up to the hotel, which I found to be very nice and plush and well taken care of. It cost me 380 yen a day to stay there, which was less then $50. This was a four-star hotel and everything was immaculate. (Don't worry, I'll have all the hotels and their locations at the end of the book.) I went up to the desk and it was very easy to register; just the normal information was necessary. I secured my stay with a credit card. There was someone behind the counter I could at least communicate with, but then again for me it was easy, because I had my young woman along so if I had a problem she was able to take care of it.

The bellhop took my luggage and up we went to the seventeenth floor. I was very impressed with the service and the overall cleanliness of the entire hotel; I strongly recommend this as your preferred place to stay if you travel to Nanning. The first thing I noticed in the room was that you must insert your door key card into a slot on the wall and keep it there for the electrical to work. The room was very spacious and nicely decorated; there was a bar and a small refrigerator that had most everything you might need. Of course, it cost extra, but it was pennies compared to what you would pay in the U.S. The bathroom was also stocked with many of the things you would use every day, and they wash your clothes and have them back to you that afternoon. If I had known this earlier I wouldn't have brought anything but a few pair of pants and shirts and antiperspirant and cologne; everything else was provided, and my luggage would have been even more available for souvenirs.

After looking around the hotel I found out that the first floor has a business center where you can make international calls, and you can pay six yen to get online and use the Internet. They also have a nice lobby bar where you can get a good assortment of drinks; the only things I found of interest to me on the menu, though, were Pabst beer and Coca-Cola. The hotel also has two restaurants on the second floor. One is for the complimentary breakfast served every morning between 7 and 10 a.m.; this consists of an all-you-can-eat buffet that is very nicely prepared, but if you're like me and want fresh eggs you must tell one of the hostesses to get it prepared for you. The other restaurant is for anytime dining, which you must pay for. I did eat there once, but of course the food was a bit more expensive than what I found later walking around in the city.

The third floor was a bar that was very nicely laid out. When I got out of the elevator on this floor, to my immediate right stood two very beautiful women in full-length gowns. They greeted me with smiles and giggles, and one of them walked me down the hall to the area where the drinks were served. Along the hall were more young ladies dressed in hotel uniforms; they were spaced about ten feet apart, and they were also very beautiful. Then I was escorted into the bar area, where they were playing music videos, and there were tables of at least thirty young women giggling and playing cards. At this time I was with my girl so I didn't pay them too much attention. When everything was said and done, the entire stay there for two weeks worked out to just over $700. I found this to be very inexpensive for this quality and service, and considering the price of this type of hotel in the States, it was very cheap.

Nanning is mostly composed of older dwellings. As I walked around most of the stores I noticed they all used roll-up doors; they weren't very big, and handled only small items. They sold just about everything you can imagine, though. I was fortunate to visit in July because this is the best time of the season for fruit and vegetables, which were sold everywhere you looked. Fruit and vegetable stands were scattered all over every street, and I couldn't see anything that didn't look just-picked and ripe and ready to be eaten. Looking even further into the streets, I noticed they have no individual homes, just apartments. Everywhere I could see were apartment buildings going up to no fewer than eight floors. The streets themselves were covered with people, and everywhere you looked they were sleeping on the sidewalk, riding bikes, motorcycles, or mopeds, or just sitting around and eating.

The city was very congested, but it was really nice although as I walked every person I saw stopped and stared at me, and the women usually giggled. But each person that saw me usually smiled, and then went about his or her business. Each and every person I came in contact with was very nice and pleasant and went out of his or her way to help me do, buy, or get whatever it was that I needed help with. They have varying areas and standards of living just as all cities do, but I was welcome no matter where I went. And as we walked down each street, even sometimes late at night, we never had any problems. And the streets usually stayed full until after 1 a.m.

The city has malls, but anything and everything you want is in one building. I mean each floor has certain departments specific to what you're looking for. They rise to at least the eighth or ninth level, and you got up to each floor by escalators. I was impressed by all the items they had, just like in the States—including clothes, cosmetics, and appliances.

The products were also arranged in groups of the same items, which means the competing shop owners are side by side; you may have five different brands of televisions, each one sold by a different merchant. When you buy something here, the salesman writes you a ticket and you must pay for it somewhere else in the building, then return with the receipt. What really surprised me was if you needed it delivered, this was immediately done upon your purchase; it went straight to your location. And if installation was required, no matter what was involved, it was included in the cost of your purchase. This amazed me; it's not something seen back in the United States, at least not very often. And just as everything else there, the cost was amazingly lower for me due to the currency exchange rate; in fact, the only things I found to be similar to United States prices were gold and diamonds.

I had the pleasure of entering some of the homes that were scattered throughout the city, but I was shocked by their standard of living. First off, you cannot drink any water in China, anywhere, unless it's bottled or boiled first. This is very important to know if you don't want to spend a lot of time in the bathroom. In one apartment I visited there were three very small rooms, with no hot water, and no toilet other than a hole in the floor. The stoves were usually one or two burners like camp stoves connected to propane tanks. The beds were hard and made of wood, even in the hotel. Yet somehow these people managed to make everything work out for them in their day-to-day lives.

The cockroaches there are huge. All the ones I saw were at least three inches long and took their time moving around. Although there weren't many of them, you couldn't miss those that were there; people merely picked them up by their antennae and whipped them out the window.

The walls in most of the structures were poured cement and the electrical came down the outside of the wall and was draped across the ceiling for lighting. The outlets have 220 and 110 volts in the same outlet, and they use straight blades for the sockets with no ground plug. So you will have problems with electrical gear from the good old U.S.A., with the one side barbed so you can run the power only one way to protect you from shorts. You should buy an adapter, or if you're in a hotel they should be able to supply you with one. There is one outlet in the bathroom dedicated to shavers that will work with a little finesse.

The hotel had cable TV, and surprisingly enough they also had Internet service available. Although I found it rather slower than what I'm used to, it worked rather well. It seemed strange to me that the Chinese lacked most of the necessities that we cannot seem to live without, yet they have some modern technology in their lives that some Americans still lack. Another thing I noticed is that most of the people there have cell phones, no matter how what their standard of living was. Some of the streets I walked down had store upon store selling nothing but cell phones. And not like the stores here in the U.S., which offer maybe five to ten phones made by four different manufacturers, but hundreds of them all over each store, of every size and color. I was amazed at all the phones they had there, and I was fortunate to find out how their calling plans work. Actually, they didn't have any plans that I could see; instead, people went in and paid for whatever number of minutes they thought they needed.

I didn't venture very far from the city at all, but they don't seem to have very much in the line of things to visit. You can tell by the standard of living that there is not much tourism, and that may have prompted all the stares and smiles, as they were happy to see me. I did go up to the mountain nearby and saw some statues and shrines where a lot of the people in Nanning spend some of their time and worship or just enjoy a day in the park. And that's what it looked like to me: a big park stretching all the way up the mountain. It was very beautiful and well groomed, and at the time of my visit there was some construction going on, so they were obviously looking to make this an attraction. It featured some spectacular sites to get some nice scenic photos. From my room I took some aerial photos of the city, and even in the center of town there were a few places where I found the architecture to be very well done, and some of the walkways were set up beautifully. But in terms of attractions I guess Nanning doesn't have anything spectacular like in Beijing, which hosts the Great Wall and the imperial palace. But for me there was no need for maps or plans for any sightseeing tours, because my trip there was strictly to meet and spend time with this wonderful woman. And it worked out to be the most wonderful time of my life.

I did visit Beijing as well and found it very similar to Nanning; the only main difference was that you could tell by the buildings that the standard of living was better. The people of Beijing also had many more cars. The people there were as welcoming as in Nanning. I stayed in a five-star hotel, a little bit more expensive than in Nanning—$80 a night, to be exact, but that's still fairly reasonable. The amenities were the same except their breakfast involved obtaining a coupon that allowed you half off the price of the meal, so even with that it still cost me $12 to eat, whereas the breakfast in Nanning was free.

You can take a cab to either the wall or the palace, but from my hotel you can also walk to the palace as it's only a few short blocks. The wall is some distance from the city, and the airport is thirty minutes from Beijing, so you have to take a cab to either destination, or catch a tourist bus at the hotel. When we landed at the airport, we decided to see the wall before going to the hotel, which was a little out of the way but still more convenient for us.

I would highly recommend a trip to China, whether you go to Nanning, Beijing, Shanghai, or just stay in Guangzhou. You will have a wonderful time and stay in elaborate hotels and get service that is customer-oriented; they will do all they can to make your stay a memorable one. So pack light and have a great time, and don't forget to take a taxi. You'll see what I mean when you get there.

Well, my friend, I believe I have discussed everything you will need to be successful in your search for the woman of your dreams. This is a proven method I have used myself. It enabled me to have hundreds of women wanting to talk with and meet me for the possibility of becoming my wife. Through the course of seven months I met many of them, but I finally decided on my young woman in China. I wish you the best of luck in your search, and I know that now that you have read my book, not only are you wiser but more aware of what to do and what to watch out for on the Internet when dating. If you apply everything I have told you, you will truly be as successful as I was, and use your personality and charm to achieve happiness with the woman of your dreams.

Recommended hotels and places to eat in China

Nanning:	Hotel Jinhua No. 1 Dongge Road, Guanxi Tel. 86-771-2088888
Guangzhou:	Hotel Guangdong 339 Huanshi Dong Lu Tel. 86-20-83311666
Beijing:	Restaurant Shun Feng Fishing Village No. 43 Dong An Men St. Tel. 65245833

Chapter 11

She's Not a U.S. Citizen—
How Do I Get Her Here?

Well, the first thing I can say is congratulations. I know you had a long search, and now you're ready to be happy. But if you're reading this she must live in a country other then the United States, right? If so, read on and let me tell you what you need to do to get her here with you. Locate your local INS office if you have one near you. If you don't then you can download the form you need at the Internet site uscis.gov. Go to the forms section and look for the I-129F Petition for an Alien Fiancée and download it. Let me make this clear right away! You don't need to hire an attorney and pay a lot of money to bring her here. Yes, there is some cost involved, but an attorney could ask for 1,500 bucks. I started to do this, but after talking with a man who applied himself, I decided to fill the paperwork out and send it in myself. OK, back to where we were at. The biggest thing about this is that you need to make sure you read the instructions and check off each item as you complete it. And if a line you're filling in doesn't apply to you or her, then write N/A. They are going to look to see that all the information is filled out correctly and you don't want any delays. So take your time and write it in block letters if you don't have a typewriter available. I didn't have one either and just used a black pen.

They are also going to want a photo of her, like a passport photo, so make sure you get one before you leave her in the country she lives. I made that mistake and didn't know, and she later mailed it to me, but waiting on it caused some delays. You will also need a letter from her, signed, of her intent to come there and be with you, and her willingness to marry you. But you will also need to send a letter stating the same thing; in the instructions it's all told to you, so read it and follow it closely. Another thing you should know: information needs to be entered in this form like her name and address, and if her native language is not English you will have to fill this information in her language where they specify, so be prepared for this. I was caught off guard, but with my fiancée being able to get online using one of the messenger services, I was able to get this from her and add it in the form. You will also need a biographical background form, and this must be filled out with four copies attached to it. I'm fortunate enough to have a INS office close by, so I could go down and get all the forms there. This form is called a G-325A and you can download it from the same site, but remember, you need to send them four copies of this form! Now you will have to know where to file the papers. At the same site that is mentioned above, go to Service Centers and click on your state. This is where you need to file all your documents. What I did once when I thought I was done was to go through everything several times and make real sure it was all filled out correctly. And check the site: there is a fee for filing the paperwork with them, and they change it from time to time, so make sure you get the correct fee amount.

Here's a brief summary on what's needed taken right from the Uscis website:

- Form I-129F Petition for Alien Fiancé(e) (if your fiancé(e) has unmarried children who are under 21, they are eligible to accompany your fiancé(e), but only if they are listed on this form.)
- Evidence of your U.S. citizenship—your original U.S. birth certificate, your U.S. passport, your Certificate of Naturalization, or your Certificate of Citizenship. (Please see USCIS Form I-129F for information on the use of copies.)
- 2 Form 325A Biographic Data Sheets (one for you and one for your fiancé(e))
- One color photo of you and one of your fiancé(e) taken within 30 days of filing (please see Form I-129F for more instructions on photos).

- A copy of any divorce decrees, death certificates, or annulment decrees if either you or your fiancé(e) have been previously married.
- Proof of permission to marry if you or your fiancé(e) are subject to any age restrictions. (For instance, in some U.S. states, you must receive special permission to marry if you are under the age of 16.)

Then the next thing you need to do once everything is complete is to go down to the local post office. You'll find the best way to send it is certified mail, and I could use a document envelope and also get a return receipt when it arrived at the service center. It took me about four days to get the receipt back; shortly afterwards I received a letter confirming that they had received it. From this point on it's a waiting game. If you go to the uscis.gov site again you can go to Case Status and Processing Dates; here you can see what they are working on. By checking the processing dates, you can also set up a customer ID and password and check on the status, as it's a direct link to your file. You see, the center works on the papers in the order they receive them, I submitted mine at the end of July and they didn't get to look at mine until November. I was checking the processing dates each and every day waiting for an update, and let me tell you, there's no method or set date when they update the processing page, so check it often. What I was later upset about was the fact that there are four processing centers in the U.S. And depending on where you live you must file to one of them that services your area, right? And when I checked their sites to see what dates they were working on, I was real mad that they had surpassed my date of filing, yet I had to wait on the service center for my area, which was behind. I even went as far as calling them and wanting to know why the other centers didn't work on mine, and the woman stated that this is how it works, and you must wait your turn.

So I gave her a nice piece of my mind and hung up on her. So I wouldn't bother to call unless the processing date is after you submitted your papers by at least thirty days. It won't do any good, so don't waste your time here. But finally I received news via an email on November 2 that my application had been approved and that I would get a letter in the mail stating such. And as a matter of fact, on November 5 I received a letter that stated my petition was approved. What a sigh of relief this was, that finally after three months I had some good news to give my fiancée. You can't imagine the smile on both of our faces and actually the tears in my eyes when I told her. But I knew the battle wasn't over.

From this point I didn't know what else was going to take place before I was able to bring my wonderful woman to come and be with me. So I did some more research to find out exactly what more was needed. I wanted to add this information and made a late entry in the book so you would know the next procedures that were needed to be done. When you receive the approval letter from the Uscis they will tell you that the completed documents will be sent to the National Visa Center. Here they will process the information given to them by the INS before it goes to the consulant that you put on the Fiancée Visa Application. This can take anywhere from two to four weeks, and I was told that once they processed it and they sent it to the consultant's office, I would get a letter telling me that they were done and that it's being sent. Such a long process for this, but I knew in the end it would be well worth it. And at least they do keep you informed of each and every step regarding where your documents are and what comes next. So here I am, waiting on their letter now, but what more will I need to do, or what will she need, when it gets there to her consulant's office? Here's how it goes, The Consul will conduct security clearance procedures and then schedule an interview, much like a permanent residence interview. Your fiancée must supply pictures, a medical exam, and an affidavit of support.

Let's talk about the affidavit of support. This you can get from the Uscis website I mentioned above from the Forms section. It's form I –134 Affidavit of Support; you can download the form—it's in Adobe Acrobat so if you don't have it, go to the Adobe site and get it free. Open this form and print it out. Once again, fill it out completely and follow the instructions. Then you will need to attach a previous-year tax statement as proof of income; don't worry, you can attach a copy! Then take the completed form and the attached tax form to a notary public where they can certify the information. Your fiancée will need this when she goes to the interview. The green card interview and K-1 interview procedures are almost identical. If the Consul issues the visa to her, all the supporting documents are put in a sealed envelope for presentation to INS at the port of entry to the U.S. This same package can be used for the adjustment of status and green card application with the INS after the marriage. The fiancée has four months from the date of visa petition approval to apply for the K-1 visa at a U.S. Consulate. Although the four-month period may be extended, each extension request casts doubt on the ultimate intention to marry in the U.S. The fiancée must either marry with in the ninety-day period or leave the U.S. If the fiancée leaves prior to the expiration of the ninety-day period and returns, he or she will only be admitted for the balance of the first ninety-day period.

Such a lengthy process isn't it? And I cannot wait to finally be done with it, but I know when everything is said and done, I will be so much happier. And I will always stand by the old saying that if it comes easy, it's surely not worth it. So best of luck to you now and make sure you comfort her and talk with her everyday and let her know what's going on and that you love her. The time will drag slowly, but what we must endure to finally have and find true love is surely worth the wait and the battle. My outcome is going to be the greatest event in my life, and if you really searched and found the right woman for you, I'm sure you will feel the same. Best of luck to you and your endeavor.

Printed in the United States
28679LVS00006B/1-21